BERNANOS

His Political Thought and Prophecy

BERNANOS

His Political Thought and Prophecy

by **Thomas Molnar**

SHEED and WARD - New York

Contents

BOOKS BY BERNANOS   vii

BIOGRAPHICAL NOTE   ix

INTRODUCTION   xiii

1. "TREASON OF THE BOURGEOISIE"   1

2. "EVERYTHING IS A QUESTION OF ELITES"   22

3. "THE NEW TREASON"   40

4. "THE SILENT TOMORROW"   77

5. VICHY: "A BALLET DANCED IN A GRAVEYARD"   115

6. "MY COUNTRY IS THE CONSCIENCE OF EUROPE"   147

7. "A TOUCHSTONE OF CHRISTIANITY"   173

To the memory of my mother

Books by Bernanos

American editions of Bernanos' political essays:
  Plea for Liberty (Pantheon, 1944)
  Tradition of Freedom (Roy, 1950)
  The Last Essays (Regnery, 1955)

Political works:

  La Grande Peur des Bien-Pensants (Grasset, 1931)
  Les Grands Cimetières sous la lune (Plon, 1938)
  Scandale de la vérité (Gallimard, 1939)
  Nous autres, Français (Gallimard, 1939)
  Le Chemin de la Croix-des-Ames (Atlantica Editora, 1943–44, Rio)
  Écrits de Combat ("Problèmes Français," 2ème série, No. 5, Beyrouth, 1942)
  Lettre aux Anglais (Gallimard, 1946)
  La France contre les Robots (Robert Laffont, 1947)
  Les Enfants humiliés (Gallimard, 1949)
  La Liberté pour quoi faire? (Gallimard, 1953)
  Le Crépuscule des vieux (Gallimard, 1956)

Shorter works:

  Noël à la Maison de France (Editions des Cahiers Libres, 1930)
  Dans l'amitié de Léon Bloy (Plon, 1947)
  Reflexion sur le Cas de Conscience Français (Fontaine, 1944)
  Autobiographie (In *La Nef*, August 1948)

The more important novels of Bernanos:

  Sous le Soleil de Satan (Plon, 1926)
  Under the Sun of Satan (New York: Pantheon, 1949)

L'Imposture (Plon, 1927)
La Joie (Plon, 1929)
Joy (New York: Pantheon, 1946)
Journal d'un Curé de Campagne (Plon, 1936)
Diary of a Country Priest (New York: Macmillan, 1948)
Nouvelle Histoire de Mouchette (Plon, 1937)
Monsieur Ouine (Plon, 1946)

A Biographical Note

GEORGES BERNANOS was born in 1888, in Paris. His family was middle class, with strong nationalist and royalist convictions, although, as he wrote later, nationalist politicians were often severely criticised in the family conversations. At the turn of the century he was a pupil of the Jesuits at the Collège de Vaugirard, which the young de Gaulle also attended. Later, while a law student in Paris, Bernanos began his collaboration with right-wing publications, and became, like so many Frenchmen of his age and persuasion, a devoted follower of Charles Maurras' nationalist, royalist movement, the *Action Française*. In these pre-war years, his intense Catholic faith and fervent patriotism alike drove him to participate in street riots and political demonstrations against the Republic, as well as against "freethinker orators" and Freemason meetings. Several times arrested, he wrote his first published article in the Santé prison.

In 1913 Bernanos was appointed director of a small nationalist weekly at Rouen. There he met the young girl whom he later married, Jeanne Talbert d'Arc, whose family descended in direct line from a brother of Joan of Arc. When the war broke out, Bernanos, though not fit for service, volunteered. During the course of the war he earned several citations for bravery.

After the war, having to provide for a growing family—eventually there were six children—Bernanos accepted a position as inspector for an insurance company. On his tours of France's eastern departments, he began to write short stories and novels, "giving shape to the many figures restlessly stirring in his head." The year 1926 saw his first great success, *Sous le Soleil de Satan.* The novel was hailed by such critics as Jacques Maritain and Léon Daudet, and Bernanos greeted as the long-awaited, great Catholic novelist of his country. Encouraged by this reception, he gave up his position to devote himself to writing.

Several novels followed, among them *Joy*, for which he received the Prix Femina. Politically no longer attached to the *Action Française*, he nevertheless continued to write for the paper and stood by his friends during the turbulent period which followed the condemnation of the movement by Rome in 1926. In 1931 he published his first great polemical work, the political biography of Edouard Drumont (*La Grande Peur des Bien-Pensants*).

Although his reputation grew with every book, the years between 1930 and 1934 were difficult for the Bernanos family. In 1933 he suffered a grave motorcycle accident which crushed one leg. From then on he could only move with the help of crutches or canes. At the end of 1934 he decided to move to Majorca; a period of intense work followed, the fruit of which was the great novel, *The Diary of a Country Priest*, which was awarded the Grand Prix du Roman of the French Academy. Other books probably would have followed if the outbreak of the Spanish Civil War had not forced him to leave the island and return to France.

Deeply disillusioned with what he had seen of the Franquist rebellion, Bernanos was even more critically affected by the domestic quarrels in his homeland which foreshadowed a similar outcome. In 1938, after the publication of his anti-Franco polemical work, *Les Grands Cimetières sous la lune*, he took his family to South America. They were warmly welcomed in Brazil and settled there on the farm of Cruz-de-las-Almas, where for four years Bernanos battled in his writings and radio speeches against the Vichy regime and the German occupation, and backed the cause of General de Gaulle.

Shortly after the war Bernanos was called back to France by the Prime Minister, General de Gaulle; but the Fourth Republic was a disappointment, and Bernanos continued his denunciations of the government, the new forms of totalitarianism and the technological mentality. A sick man, he left France again for North Africa where he continued to write, lecture and warn with an extraordinary lucidity against coming disasters. In 1948, critically ill and unable to begin his projected *Life of Jesus*, he returned to France for an emergency operation at the American Hospital at Neuilly. That is where he died, on the fifth day of July.

Introduction

ACCORDING to Hans Urs von Balthasar, the author of *Le Chrétien Bernanos*, several decades will have to pass before an authoritative biography of Bernanos may be presented to the public. For one thing, many of his smaller texts have not yet appeared in print, in spite of the periodic publication since 1949 of such texts, reminiscences and notes in the *Bulletin de la Société des Amis de Bernanos*. An edition of his collected letters was to be undertaken by Albert Béguin; his death in 1957 will delay this publication. For another thing, Bernanos is too near us in time for an all-inclusive study to be devoted to his life, ideas, works and general significance. Those who were close to him, like Albert Béguin himself, felt impelled to give expression to the influence that his great and passionate figure had had on them. There are good and penetrating essays about him by Béguin, Luc Estang, Gaetan Picon and André Rousseaux, as well as the longer study by the German Catholic scholar, Urs von Balthasar; but for reasons I hope to make clear, it is natural that we should be unable as yet to understand the full measure of the man, to penetrate his soul and to estimate his impact which is growing and extending beyond Catholic circles and beyond Latin countries.

A writer usually finds several—and to him satisfactory—reasons why he should devote time and effort to his subject. Even without going deeply into the "whys" of writing a book on Bernanos, I feel I can present some valid arguments: Ber-

nanos is in the forefront, with Claudel and Mauriac, of contemporary Catholic literature in France, which, since roughly
1910, has been the equal, if not in quantity, certainly in originality and significance, of "non-Catholic" literature.[1] In this way,
Bernanos has been one of the major influences on a generation
of novelists and has decisively shaped French Catholic sensibilities, particularly in the post-1945 era.[2] However, while
penetrating to the very core of Catholic problems and spiritual
life, while becoming the novelist of the sacerdotal soul, Bernanos was also—before Mauriac and with a different orientation—a Catholic intellectual who was also an *engagé*, fighting
for causes, never avoiding a battle and accepting the harsh
consequences of a series of unpopular opinions, attitudes and
actions.

These reasons would be more than enough for devoting a
book to Bernanos. The man, who had found so soon the truth
of his soul, but who found his career with such difficulty, and
fame only when he was more than forty years of age, stands
before us today as a major literary, even cultural figure. *The
Diary of a Country Priest* has become a classic; his play, *Dialogue des Carmelites*, with Poulenc's music, is a successful
opera; his *Les Grands Cimetières sous la lune*, written out of
his indignation with the civil war in Spain, is the most forceful
political pamphlet of the century.

And still, there are greater and more valid reasons to speak
of Bernanos today. If such a thing could be at all stated of a
Christian who believes that he is part of the mystical body of
Christ, Bernanos could be called an "alienated man," somewhat
in the sense in which Kierkegaard, Nietzsche and Kafka were
alienated. In reality, such a man is the least alienated of all; the
fact that among modern robots, the de-personalized men, a
man like Bernanos is *free*, makes us believe that he is a saboteur,
a strange and backward figure, refusing to join us on our terms.

Thus "alienated," in the case of Bernanos, means a human
being with exceptional unity of purpose, intellectual integrity,

moral courage and spiritual elevation, but not at all in the
sense of a delicate, fragile, ascetic figure. Bernanos was a robust
man—his physical misfortunes were always caused by reckless-
ness, accidents, perhaps by his terrific fits of fury. Nor did
he believe that he was in any sense saintly; he was passionate,
violent, full of vigor, charging his enemies like a bull. But he
had other qualities which made of him a stumbling block for
the wise men of this world, the important ones, lay or ecclesiastic, the respectable ones, bourgeois or socialist. These qualities are those of an essentially simple, childlike man. The sophisticated analyst of the soul, the writer who knew the secret
of impostor priests, innocently wise virgins, and dried-up
aristocrats, the restless traveler who so easily adjusted his
vision to new landscapes, the public accuser and tireless Cassandra—was a simple man without a system, without an aca-
demically sanctioned philosophy.

He *lived* instead. Bernanos had the immediate realism of the
French peasant, his concrete feel of life, his understanding of
and respect for what *is*. This does not mean something sullen,
something that never raises its head; it means, rather, to have
roots in life—whether in France or in Brazil—an understanding
of human beings undistorted by an ideology, or simply by
pessimism and optimism, an understanding which accounts for
the incredible insights of the young curé of Ambricourt into
the depths of the souls around him. And it shows an almost
naive, good-humored satisfaction with life because it is always
fascinating.

Drama was certainly not absent from his life. In his youthful
years, he was a street fighter among the right-wing *camelots
du roi*, battling with the police and spending nights in jail. He
spent the war years in the army, and in the following years
struggled in a world where his talents and independence of
mind could not easily be exchanged for a livelihood. They
were years lived as an intellectually solitary man, revising some
earlier beliefs and loyalties—not as a renegade, but as a sud-

denly enlightened man. He suffered deeply for his beloved France, and in the short years between his return to France and his death fought, once more, to open the eyes of his countrymen. It was a life full of work, travel and passionate speeches. Throughout these years the accompanying note is an all-consuming violence, not for personal gain or success, but for truth as he saw it: "If I am violent," he wrote in 1939 to his Brazilian friend, Amoroso Lima, "it is to spare others the need to be violent." And in 1947: "People say," he wrote, "that Bernanos is never pleased about anything or anyone. When the righteous were wishing success to the crusade of our good neighbor, Señor Franco, he wrote *Les Grands Cimetières sous la lune,* and protested against being called democratic. Now that all righteous are each more democratic than the others, he still proclaims himself Catholic, and no more democratic than before. A peculiar fellow, that Bernanos."[3]

This quotation and the "violence" of which Bernanos speaks in his letter to Amoroso Lima refer to his political opinions and writings. But it is rather difficult to mention in the same sentence the name of Bernanos and the term "political." Nothing was farther from his impatient and burning temperament than the meticulousness of the news analyst or the politician's maneuvers between parties, programs and committees. His domain was, rather, the philosopher's insight and the artist's intuition, the social critic's scorn and wrath, and the prophet's words predicting doom. Why should one, then, speak of the *political thought* of Bernanos?

Urs von Balthasar states in his book that Bernanos' primary interest was "the human person and his integrity; the question of what political system promotes the values of the person was, for him, of secondary importance."[4] Perhaps in another age he would have remained far from politics and political preoccupations. Our time, however, is such that men like Bernanos are inevitably drawn toward an examination and a critique of the *collective conscience* (of a nation, a society, a class or civilization), and this conscience is inevitably expressed through political channels and political terminology. Hence the unbreakable link today between the man of conscience and the community which holds his hopes and fears, his commitment, captive.

This was the case of Bernanos. As he confessed on two or three occasions, he was irresistibly attracted to the political phenomenon—to the point where he was compelled to set aside his literary work, a decision he never ceased deploring, yet could not reverse. He and his readers were, however, compensated; he had the same human grasp of politics as of the characters in his novels. The political animal comes alive in his essays and pamphlets; his innermost secrets are probed as is the black heart of Monsieur Ouine or the supernatural joy of Chantal de Clergerie. And this is true not only of the political animal in his individuality but also of a nation or a class—the corps of high Army officers, diplomat-priests, or the pressure group of shop-keepers. They all are given life; they are impersonated and made protagonists in a drama which is the very core of politics. The extraordinary range of images in which the individual and collective actors are depicted, the dialogues they conduct, the greed, the bafflement, the interests, the corruption, the generosity which mark their consciences, show Bernanos, the writer, at his best. But it also shows him towering above most political writers and puts him in the same class with the great actors and commentators of great events, de Gaulle and Churchill.

What makes the case of Bernanos particularly striking (and what served as the original inspiration of this book) is that *his political experience shows an extraordinary transformation under the pressure of his religious faith.* Simply stated: his charity curbed his political temperament at a certain moment when all those with similar convictions and principles and similar ideological background adhered more fully than before to an extremist position. The fact that Bernanos overcame what I shall call in a later chapter the "fascist temptation" is an event which has not been given the attention it deserves, probably because the world was soon to witness more spectacular denunciations of a previously embraced political faith by men like Silone, Koestler and Chambers. But we can never think of Bernanos as an ex-fascist or a potential fascist. Naturally, there are readers and commentators who stamp him as a reactionary on the basis of his earlier years. They point to his participation among the *camelots du roi*, his membership in the *Action Française*, his admiration for the anti-Semitic Drumont and his friendly rapport with Maurras and Daudet. There are critics who refer to his earlier writings (*La Grande Peur des Bien-Pensants*, in particular), his nostalgia for the France of Joan of Arc and of "peasant and knights" and his sharp criticism of the modern "imbeciles," technocrats and progressives, as indisputable symptoms of a "fascist" mentality. But the objective witness, with even a little of the sympathy he can hardly refuse him, will look back on the Bernanos of the *Diary*, *Les Grands Cimetières sous la lune* and his wartime writings, and will discover the key to a man who overcame a far more formidable temptation than political extremism: the *temptation of despair*. In this age when literature, art and politics find the ultimate meaning in meaninglessness, when intellectual fatigue engulfs the private study and the public place, we are struck by something constant in his spiritual structure, and we must call it his *living faith*.

This was the source of his independence, even vis-à-vis the Church. Did he not say: "I follow truth wherever it leads me, and profess it regardless of the consequences." Bernanos had the highest regard for the clergy and its individual members; witness to this were his teachers, then Dom Besse, the abbé Pézeril, Father Tauzin and many others. But this did not stop him from denouncing publicly all the "Eminences, bishops and archbishops" who closed their eyes to the atrocities in Spain or blessed Mussolini's ruthless campaign in Abyssinia. Since he was a Christian, at home in his Father's House, he considered it his duty to uncover the evils infesting Christian integrity, the stinking wounds in the soul of a priest who had lost his faith (abbé Cénabre), or to probe the hallucinations of another who caused scandal by the startling manifestations of his mysticism (abbé Donissan).

Yet, Bernanos was not at all an "angry man," a ruthless critic; outside his charity, which transpires even through his invectives, the main feature of his personality was humanness and joy. I have said how securely he was rooted in life, in God's world; his joy grew out of these roots and was, as a result, a way of looking at the world and at himself in it. This unity of his being, the conviction that he had rights and duties in this world with which he felt an organic kinship, adds a particular flavor to his role as a public figure. Not as a politician, for at no time was he one; but as a Frenchman, with the weight of history and tradition and the wings of the future. A participant in his nation's destiny, not a listless voting machine, but as a man who felt in his blood and fibers the slightest motions of the communal body and felt, hoped and suffered with it.

It must be stressed at this point that Bernanos occupies a unique position among the modern critics of society. He was not an *existentialist* recalling his fellow human beings to the austere task of choosing a meaning in an absurd universe; he was not a *neo-humanist* interested in the cultivation of values; he was not a *romantic* denouncing the industrial age for its ugliness and narrow imagination; and he was not a *philosopher of culture* of the Spengler-Toynbee school, measuring and comparing the phases of civilizations and situating the twentieth century on their gigantic graph. To be sure, his remarks touched upon all these aspects of the day's cultural criticism; but his originality was elsewhere: all the other analyses of the modern world have an intellectualist approach by which they are themselves symptoms of what they examine and criticise. They are inseparable from the social and cultural milieu which supplies them with the data they study, the methods they use, the frame of reference and even the ideal they favor. With some simplification, one might say that the systems of contemporary culture-critics and social critics are re-arrangements of the given elements, not their fundamental transformations.

The case of Bernanos is different. He was not an intellectualist thinker and he was not systematic. He did not proceed from firmly and rationally established premises; he did not equip his arguments with the weapons of philosophical analysis, nor was his reasoning surrounded with the guarantees of a rigorous logic. In his essays, Luc Estang writes, "enthusiastic vaticination frequently wins out. His eloquence sets sail, his thought dilutes itself. Bernanos' essays are not distinguished by their dialectical rigor, but by the passion which animates them."[5] Yet, these remarks do not do justice to Bernanos, the thinker, because it is much more than passion that drove his pen. The simplest way to put it is to say that he understood the *spirit* of the phenomena which form the object of his great likes and dislikes; he saw them *sub specie humanitatis* and penetrated their innermost significance. When he attacks the conquest of technology, for example, it is not a carefully documented study which would destroy the flavor of the subject, so to speak, and neutralize it under our intelligence-directed attention. Rather, he attacks it in its roots—in the dead sediments it leaves in the soul, in the way it affects our basic attitudes, our relationship with God and men. In his pleadings for freedom, for individuality, for life as conceived by God, Bernanos does not impress by the number of his arguments, but by the depth of his penetration; to give another example, it is not the duel of man versus the state which he describes—any competent political scientist would do this, but the struggle of two principles—and yet how concretely presented—which seem, under his pen, to contradict each other and to have contradicted each other from all eternity, in the very plan of Creation.

The personality and thinking of Bernanos was, then, unique because of his blend of temperament, sensibility and convictions. Few manage to generate enough fire to heat themselves at its side, let alone the fire which was burning in him. It is a cause for rejoicing that such a man lived in this century, and may have balanced with his merits much of its sin and corruption.

NOTES

1. Among the young Catholic writers who have achieved, since the war, national and, in some cases, international reputation, let me mention Jean Cayrol, Paul-André Lesort, Gilbert Cesbron, Luc Estang, and the poet, Pierre Emmanuel. Among the philosophers and critics Etienne Borne, Jean Guitton, Albert Béguin, Luc Estang, Gabriel Marcel, Daniel-Rops.
2. In a recent poll of French female students, Bernanos was found to lead the list of preferred authors.
3. *Last Essays* (Chicago: Regnery, 1955), p. 262.
4. *Le Chrétien Bernanos* (Ed. du Seuil, 1956), p. 502.
5. *Présence de Bernanos* (Plon, 1947), p. 193.

1 *"Treason of the Bourgeoisie"*

BERNANOS was in no sense a politician. He did not have one eye on his own future platforms, saving for himself a way out of the situations he tried to bring about, but immersed himself in everything he did; detachment, cursory treatment and theoretical discussion were not traits of his personality. For him, forty-some years of active life were not cut up into slices: slices of Maurrassism, the World War, Poincaré-era, right-wing leagues, Spanish Civil War and Popular Front. In his case it is no mere stereotyped expression to say that he had an inner unity which always turned the entire personality in the direction which seemed the most absorbing at the time, with which it might commune, to which it might respond.

This fact, characteristic of him, will help us understand his whole life and the positions he took with regard to personalities and events. Although, as he matured in years and experience, his political ideas and attitudes were less and less typical of his generation and his milieu, it will not be difficult to understand them for this reason: his absolute sincerity was a kind of compass built into his moral system and helps explain his errors and exaggerations as well as his sound judgments and logical deductions. To those who doubt his capacity for sound judgment and logic, who always call into question the sanity of the solitary holders of truth, one can only answer that the political evolution of Bernanos proves an ability to give up untenable situations, to learn from facts and observations, to rise from the singular to the general and to confess faults of judgment. It is true: his passionate nature tended to veil the down-to-earth quality of his observations; he was neither a systematic thinker, nor a practical man; but on the level at which things made sense to *him*, he had a power of insight not ordinarily given to politicians or statesmen living in close contact with events and responsible for their shaping.

His kind of moral courage is rare among politicians and statesmen or the simple party member. After his youthful involvement in the *Action Française*, Bernanos never allowed his freedom to be chained to party organizations, leagues or political pressure groups, and certainly not to attitudes which appeared expedient at the time. While in Maurrassian circles pure doctrine was polluted by various power considerations, Machiavellian moves and personal intrigues, Bernanos not only stood aloof from the trend of the movement, but even marked his freedom by open gestures towards the defeated or attacks on the triumphant. These gestures did not signify scorn or defiance, and they were by no means calculated; they emerged from the depth of his conviction and were fashioned by an uncompromising integrity.

An even more fundamental point must be made about Bernanos' way of looking at the world.

Much is said and written in our mid-century psychological literature about the child, his world and his needs, but one has the impression, somehow, that the point of all the concern and preoccupation is to steal childhood away from children by integrating them into the adults' world. As in seventeenth-century paintings where children can be seen in the form of grown-ups on a reduced scale, many of our educators and child-psychologists treat childhood as a preparatory stage for certain adult performances; we hear them talk about learning the "democratic processes," of participating in "group activities," of decisions in the classroom situation," of criticism passed on their "parents' behavior." Rapidly, under the impact of child psychology and the adult-imposed organization of teen-age life, the world of children, a world of daily renewed marvels, of communion with the magic dimension of life, of solitary brooding and the delights found in playmates, is absorbed in the grey continuum of the "average citizen's" existence.

We must, I feel, mention the imposture perpetrated today on the child, in order to penetrate the world of Bernanos. It is difficult, naturally, to picture the child behind the robust, broad-shouldered man with features so deeply furrowed by a life spent in passionate combat. Yet, the child is everywhere in him, the spirit of childhood, its simplicity and spontaneity. His was the kind of soul to which Jesus referred when He said: "Be like children," and "Let the children come to me."

What is Bernanos' relationship to childhood? His biographer and trusted friend, Albert Béguin, writes of him: "The division of the Bernanosian world is not between good ones and bad ones; it is between saints who have remained loyal to childhood, and the despairing ones who have lost it."[1] Bernanos himself says it with different words: "If I no longer have the child's purity, I have at least retained a kind of natural simplicity."[2]

What do these terms mean: "childlike" and "natural simplicity" in the company of "saintliness" and "despair"? Béguin was right in dividing what he called "the Universe of Bernanos" in two parts, and also right in symbolizing one by the figure of the saint and of the child. Reading the works of Bernanos—the novels and pamphlets, the diaries and the speeches—one is aware of a world crystallized around two kinds of people lined up, as it were, for battle. People on one side are variously referred to as children, Christians, saints, free men, Frenchmen; on the other side are the impostors, the phonies, the imbeciles, the self-righteous, the hypocrites, the robots.

It is not Bernanos' way to build rigid categories in a Manicheistic world of sharply separated blacks and whites. All of his Christians are certainly not among the "good ones"; on the contrary, as he expects very much from those whose shoulders he burdens with mankind's integrity and honor, he hates none more than the impostor priest (the abbé Cénabre of his *L'Imposture*) in whom the vein of childhood has dried up. If, on the other hand, one gets acquainted with the curé of Ambricourt (in *The Diary of a Country Priest*), the contrast immediately appears, not merely between the good priest and the bad, but between the natural simplicity of the first and the tortured sophistication of the second. In this way the child appears as the foundation of man, his communion with the spiritual sphere, the primeval being not yet weaned from God; more simply, the child in man is the source of positive life, of unending hope, of truthfulness and a sense of honor.

Although on these pages we are going to deal with the non-fictional writings of Bernanos, the unity of inspiration of the man as a novelist and as a prophet is so evident that we must turn first to his novels if we wish to understand his view of the world, because there is a constant correspondence between the characters in his novels and the principal personalities in his field of actual observation.

The world of Bernanos' novels reflects his main preoccupation: what is the position of the saint in a world teeming with the most complicated, the most sophisticated forms of evil? But, first of all, who is a saint? and what is evil? What happens when these two poles of spirituality come into contact? These are the problems that Bernanos pursues in all his works—in his political writings as well as in his novels.

The spiritual man is not a strictly religious phenomenon; he is, rather, the man with a positive life whose being is heavy with the weight of God in him. He may be a simple peasant, a public figure, a young girl or a priest; in each case his life is centered on an Existence that is infinitely higher than his own, which gently urges him along the road of suffering and sacrifice, leading, ultimately, to Golgotha. To each of these figures may be applied Albert Béguin's words: "The destiny of the priest [in Bernanos' novels] is suffering and temporal failure . . . because he is a spiritual being in a world which distrusts spirituality."[3]

But if the life of the spiritual man is derision and defeat, he is also the supremely perplexing obstacle which obstructs the sinner's progression. In old Christian writers sin was surrounded by awe, with a resulting erotic flavor of temptation; for their grandchildren sin became a fascinating aspect of the human adventure, an almost scientific product of a godless age. Sin was, for a Racine, a dramatic step, the forbidden fruit of a slowly maturing strategy, a note of exclamation after a passionate dialogue with God; in the novels of Mauriac and Graham Greene sin is part of a desolate landscape or of an oppressive climate, and the sinner himself is a sad and pitiable character who omits from his reckoning the power of grace and its unexpected visits.

Bernanos' sinners are all in a state of advanced spiritual corruption. The soul, absorbed in self-contemplation, shrinks continually until it is stripped of all the elements which originally composed its mysterious chemistry. This is a half-conscious process, but the victim turns away wilfully from the spectacle he offers. Even when he can no longer deceive himself, when, panic-stricken, he finds himself in the cold night of unbelief, he does not give up. He tries to bargain: "After all," abbé Cénabre keeps repeating to himself, "I have lost only God which means that I have lost nothing. I must admit, however, that I had organized my life around this hypothesis . . . God is necessary for my habits, my work, my status as a priest, I shall, therefore, continue acting as if God existed. I must make this choice once and for all."[4]

Cénabre, the central character of L'Imposture, is a priest and a man of superior intellect. The drama, in his case, erupts with

a particular force; his imposture spreads with the speed of an
infectious disease; as the poison works in his system, he disin-
tegrates spiritually, intellectually, and even physically. The
book he writes no longer has the qualities that the world used
to admire; he becomes listless and negligent, and his formerly
meticulous neatness yields to a sudden desire for external degradation.

Or take Monsieur de Clergerie, the pedantic historian in *Joy*,
whose sole great ambition is to be elected to the Academy. Does
he defy God? By no means. But, in the words of the saintly
abbé Chevance, he is "opaque": God is not visible through
him. His little manias, his constant complaints about the heat
and about his nerves, are innocent only in appearance; in fact,
he had let a young wife die of despair at his side and now pre-
pares to sacrifice a daughter to a second marriage which would
promote his election. He surrounds himself with souls as dry
as his own and with vicious servants who thrive in the ambiguous atmosphere of the house. As one of them remarks:
"Nobody here has the courage of good or evil."

The same may be said of the Count's family in *The Diary of
a Country Priest*. For years the Countess had been living in the
darkest night of the soul; she had lost a son and, by a morbid
attachment to the dead, alienated the living. Her husband chases
the servant-girls and governesses; her daughter hates her and
plans to kill herself in order to bring scandal and further deso-
lation on the house.

The examples could be multiplied, but the central preoccupation is always the same: the priest as a saint (Donissan in *Under
the Sun of Satan*, the curé of Ambricourt in the *Diary*, abbé
Chevance in *L'Imposture*), and then the negative priest, the
anti-priest, the whited sepulchre (Cénabre, Monsieur Ouine,
Doctor La Pérouse). No other author has treated the figure
of the priest in such a deep yet nuanced manner. As a Balzac
of the sacerdotal world, Bernanos explores the priest's life, his

inner conflicts and external conditions, his place at the cross-roads where the ways of God and men meet.

To the unity of the characters there corresponds, in Bernanos' novels, a certain unity of the topic. The desiccated soul of one man infects the souls and actions of others; sin is a dynamic reality, living a life of its own, eating itself into the tissue of being. It has such an impact that only a saint may force it to a halt and eventually reverse it. The economy of salvation functions as a well-ordered plan.

The man of God makes his presence felt by his extraordinary lucidity. The young curé of Ambricourt, the abbé Chevance or Chantal de Clergerie are people with little experience of the world. They are shy and disarmingly naive; they stumble along the path of everyday routine where even a child would walk unguided. Abbé Chevance, an elderly man, had not even been entrusted with a parish after his awkwardness in the first. The curé in *The Diary of a Country Priest* is an idealistic freshman among the tough and suspicious peasants who obstruct his well-meaning enterprises. And Chantal is only an extremely young girl, exhausted by the tasks of running a household. They know no evil; they could say, with the curé of Ars, that all they know about sin is what they learned from the lips of sinners.

Yet these three are capable of forcing the most hardened carapace to break and uncover the palpitating soul underneath. Cénabre before Chevance, the psychiatrist La Pérouse in Chantal's presence, the Countess cornered by the curé of Ambricourt become like fragile children bathed in a mother's strict but immense charity. In these scenes of confrontation, which are, beyond any doubt, Bernanos' best, the sinner has all the advantages of intelligence, fame and authority. That he yields, step by step, is nothing if not the work of living faith. An incredible transformation takes place; the young priest or the young girl seem to grow gradually old and weary, as if they were struggling with a tremendous burden which they have taken from the sinner's back; but they never weaken. Their purity absorbs the world's wickeness. They carry out "the saint's duty, the duty for which he was born: the salvation of weak souls."

We see now that the world for Bernanos is a perpetual drama between those whom I have called "desiccated souls" and those "heavy with the weight of God." The greatness of Bernanos and the significance of his continued presence in our world derive from the fact that he was no mere observer of this drama, but a participant, somewhat in the same way as the curé of Ambricourt participates in the tragedy unfolding in the Count's household; by the grace of God he has a strangely incisive vision, a lucidity which allows him to go immediately to the essence of things and people on whose behalf he then bears testimony.

But whether it is the curé of Ambricourt, Chantal de Clergerie or Joan of Arc herself, for whom Bernanos had a special veneration, it is always the child in these men and women who saves their fellow human beings and, if necessary, suffers martyrdom for them. This is true of Bernanos himself insofar as we may consider his work a unique and passionate participation in the drama of our time. The force he displays in these writings derives from the conviction that only a total sincerity may cut through the fat layers of hypocrisy and bad faith which hide truth from men's eyes. And this sincerity, as well as the courage to make of it his chief instrument, he derives, in turn, from the memory of himself as a child, from the promises he must have made to himself in long solitary hours that he would always remain true to a sensitive and delicate child's soul. "When I take up my pen and begin to write," he confessed at the age of forty-seven, "my childhood emerges right away, a childhood which had nothing extraordinary, which was like anybody else's, and from which I draw all that I write as from a source of endless dreams."[5]

As a child, Bernanos was rather timid and retiring, and in the elementary grades he frequently suffered from the cruel "insouciance" of his classmates. Certain cliché-ridden schools of modern psychology would no doubt attribute the aggressiveness of the later Bernanos to the suppressed vitality and self-expression in his early years; his life-long fidelity to the monarchist ideal and his militancy in right-wing political organizations would, I imagine, also be explained by the frustrations of the child. But, of course, Bernanos was far too rich and complex a personality to fit neat psychological categories; he gave the impression of great interior balance. He had a huge laughter and comic sense and was capable of entertaining, with a true Gallic onslaught of words, a company of brilliant talkers; he was capable too of listening with serenity to those who came to him for advice or with confidences. Although Mauriac has called him "a wild bird hurling itself against the bars of a materialistic age," it would be a mistake to imagine him as a carping, whining fellow, a professional non-conformist.

Few of his professors developed any liking for him since French was the only subject which really interested him. His compositions were carefully done, already a conscious preparation for the life of a writer. "If I do not read or write, things go badly for me," he wrote to one of his teachers. More and more, his life was organized around the future literary vocation; he devoured, lying on the floor of his father's study, the complete works of Balzac, Bourget and the early Zola. In a letter to his fiancée, sent from the front in 1914, he wrote: "When I shall be quite unable to arrange my novels in my head and let my dear phantoms come and go there at will, you will know that your poor friend lives no more."

Writing, however, was not his only ambition. He could not think of it otherwise than as an instrument of combat. He was sixteen years old when he informed his favorite French teacher, a priest, that he would himself have chosen to be a priest had he felt called by God; and then he added, "but a layman has possibilities of fighting where a priest has not."

What did young Bernanos want to fight? What was the position of a middle-class boy in the first decade of the nineteenth century?

Bernanos' early years, like those of every Frenchman of his generation, were stamped by the Dreyfus case, Maurrassian agitation, Church-State conflict and finally World War I. All of these issues provoked great intellectual, social and national passions at the time; most of them are still fought over in France, dividing Left and Right. It will be impossible to understand any of Bernanos' subsequent attitudes unless we consider the political realities of his adolescent years. And since we are dealing with a nation in which political movements and party ideologies are fed to an extraordinary degree from the sources of the past, it will be necessary to go back one or two generations. We must first see how the liberal-democratic stream of the nineteenth century had clashed with the conservative-Catholic tradition of the country's majority.

THE REVOLUTION

There is a recurrent theme in all the writings of Bernanos, but especially in his early works; it is the theme of treason. It was a common term, a logical conclusion of the reasoning characteristic of right-wing thought and literature, because the conservative-traditionalist mentality cannot conceive of changes unfavorable to its ideals except by conspiracy, treason and dramatic breaks with the past. The first "treasonable act" went back, in the eyes of right-wing families like the one to which Bernanos belonged, to the French Revolution.

Not exactly to 1789, though; as Bernanos liked to repeat, the Count of Chambord, last descendant of the Bourbon line, had told a delegation of workers when his hopes were still high for his return to the throne: "Whenever you wish, we shall resume together the great movement of 1789." In the eyes of the Pretender and of the royalists, 1789 was brought about by the government which needed the support of the Third Estate in order to force the first two, and especially the nobility, to accept their share of the financial burdens. The real treason began a few years later, in 1793, when the king was executed and when, with him, the last obstacle was removed before the complete victory of the capitalist class.

In Bernanos' view, the history of the nineteenth century had been a series of further victories of this class, resulting in the consolidation of their power and in the apotheosis of selfishness, exploitation, and shortsighted direction of the nation's destiny. "The split in the modern world," he was to write later, "is not that of 1789; it runs along the line of treason by the bourgeoisie: 1848 represents a much more decisive cleavage than 1789, because that is when the great imposture saw the light of day. Until 1848 the bourgeoisie had been content with a morality of its own fabrication; after that, prompted by the fear of the lower classes, it began to use the language of Christians."

It was a representative view. Many groups, both Left and Right, opposed the bourgeois Republic. The largest of these was the Roman Catholics.

"Catholic" here does not mean one monolithic group, a unified position without significant dissent. In a basically Catholic community, opinion was divided and Catholics belonged to both the "intransigent" and the "liberal" trends. It is a division which is valid even today: Catholic intellectuals may still be classified in this way although, of course, there are many whose mind and allegiance are divided on the issue, and the positions, especially on the plane of practical politics, are not easy to disentangle.

LIBERAL CATHOLICS

Liberal Catholic thought was, for a long time, a rather weak plant. It insisted, with the abbé Lamennais in the 1830's, that the

Church separate itself from the monarchist position. A pioneer in advocating this idea, Lamennais further insisted that the Church, freed from the burdens of this uncomfortable alliance, should make common cause with the "people," the awakening proletariat. As his disciples, Lacordaire and Ozanam, wrote later in their newspaper, *L'Ere Nouvelle:* "There are only two forces left in the country: Jesus Christ and the people. Their alliance will be the salvation of France."

Many Catholics shared this view, although they were the isolated ones, with none of the organizational power of either the Church or society behind them. In his novel, *Germinal,* Zola puts the following words in the mouth of the abbé Ranvier: "The rich have taken the place of God and govern in His place . . . If the poor people joined forces with the clergy, what power would the Pope suddenly have! He would command the immense mass of the workers. In a week the usurpers would be driven out, people would be compensated according to their merits, and the laws of work would regulate universal happiness."[6]

Was this view characteristic of the members of the clergy? Certainly in a small sector of it, especially among those country priests of modest origin who understood both the condition of the peasant and worker class and the supernatural tasks of the Church. We find this sentiment expressed in Bernanos' *The Diary of a Country Priest,* where the curé of Torcy recalls the early years of his priesthood. It was shortly after the promulgation of the Encyclical *Rerum Novarum* by Pope Leo XIII, which formulated the Church's official stand on the social question: "Take the famous *Rerum Novarum,*" he tells his young protégé, the curé of Ambricourt, "Nowadays you read it calmly, almost distracted, as a Lenten regulation. At the time, my boy, we felt as if the earth had been shaking under our feet. What enthusiasm! I was then curé of Norenfontes, in the mining country. The simple idea that work was not merchandise subject to the law of supply and demand, that one may not speculate with wages and with human lives as with wheat, or sugar, or coffee, stirred up our consciences, you may believe me! For having explained it to my parishioners, the rich peasants called me a Socialist, and had me transferred to Montreuil as a disgrace. Disgrace! Who cared?"[7]

INTRANSIGENT CATHOLICS

In the country at large, however, and particularly in the rural areas dominated by aristocratic landowners and prosperous farmers, the episcopate and the lower clergy alike maintained positions inherited from the pre-revolutionary old regime, that is a monarchistic loyalty, aggressively anti-republican. They were strengthened in their intransigence by Pope Pius IX's *Syllabus of Modern Errors* (1864), by the newspaper *L'Univers* of the brilliant Veuillot and later, after 1892, by another newspaper, *La Libre Parole*, of the nationalist, anti-Semitic Edouard Drumont.

Powerful ammunition as the *Syllabus* and these newspapers were, the point must be emphasized that the French clergy of the time were not members of a uniquely reactionary Church. They expressed, in their own way, the feeling of the *majority* of the population, dismayed by the disappearance of old France under the hammer-blows of modern economic forces. This must be placed in the context of the feeling of humiliation and revenge after the 1870 defeat, the fear of emboldened capitalism with its exploitation on a new scale and the scandals involving Republican politicians. The Republican regime was known for its anti-clericalism, its "progressive" views and its hostility to the Army as a feudal stronghold.

In other words, the conflict of interests, traditions and convictions was practically *built into* the institutions, the public life and the basic attitudes of the new-born Third Republic. Alternately on the defensive or on the offensive, the "conservative" and "liberal" Catholics attacked each other and the State, according to which side the latter was favoring at the moment. And each time that some sort of truce could have been established, a new event came not merely to thwart an eventually peaceable evolution, but to crystallize further the existing antagonistic positions.

Let us see, for example, what happened to one attempt at a rapprochement, the so-called *Ralliement*. Pope Leo XIII, alarmed by the progress of the Socialist parties in Italy and France, considered it in the interest of both countries and of the Church to relieve the hostility between Catholics and their governments. Accordingly he advised the overwhelmingly monarchistic Catholic elite in France to find a modus vivendi with the de facto Republic. The leaders of the conservative Catholic forces did not see—or did not want to see—that their active participation in the affairs of the Republic, and eventually the formation of a Catholic party, would be an excellent move for checking the growth of socialism, or, at least, for establishing a long overdue dialogue with the working class and its political representatives. The majority of Catholic leadership rejected the compromise between their loyalty to monarchy and collaboration with the Republican state. (When, for example, the Count Albert de Mun, who favored such a compromise, suffered an electoral defeat, his fellow-Catholics on the monarchist right-wing were the first to applaud.)

At this point, a scandal of historic dimensions shattered all hopes that the French Catholics would support the Republic. The Dreyfus scandal started as a triumphant issue for the nationalist-conservative forces. Dreyfus, a Jewish army captain, was found guilty of treason by a military court; the Republican Cabinet was discredited for neglecting the nation's defense secrets. It ended with Dreyfus' exoneration and in a complete defeat of the conservatives, a defeat so clear that it could never be acknowledged as such. The Captain and his case became a precious instrument in the hands of the successive governments from 1900 to 1914, an instrument by which they could proceed with the separation of Church and State, the laicization of the educational system, and the democratization of the Army, which was purged of officers of monarchistic inclination and of openly professed Catholic faith. No wonder that Jacques Bainville, a rightist historian, wrote later about the Dreyfus case that it became "a political affair which enabled the Radicals to regain power and the Socialists to slip in behind them."

DRUMONT

The most eloquent propagandist of the right-wing position was Edouard Drumont. Young Bernanos was brought up in close contact with his ideas, and his influence accompanied him throughout his life. Drumont's views were elaborated in *La Fin d'un monde* and *La France juive* and in innumerable articles in the newspaper, *La Libre Parole*, the main organ of the anti-Dreyfusards. Bernanos' father read Drumont's paper regularly, finding there the daily dose of invectives against Jews, Freemasons, Clemenceau's Radicals, German infiltration and the anti-Church laws of the Prime Minister, the ex-seminarian, Combes.

Bernanos' deep sympathy for Drumont originates, of course, in a similarity of convictions. But as the object of youthful admiration, as an embodiment of the early Bernanosian ideal of a man fighting even after the cause had been lost, Drumont's impact remained deeply engraved in the soul of Bernanos. In fact, I would venture to say that he turned back to Drumont when he felt that the final break with Maurras was inevitable. The former, in addition to an arsenal of ideas from which Bernanos and his confreres had been supplied in their youth, possessed a spiritual dimension, charity, goodness, and a peasant-like attachment to the soil, all of which were lacking—at least in Bernanos' estimation—in Maurras.

Drumont's influence on Bernanos and his generation makes

it necessary for us to turn to *La Grande Peur des Bien-Pen-sants** (written in 1931) before dealing with his youthful writings. There is little originality in these texts. It is also obvious that Bernanos was, at the time, preoccupied with a purely literary career. If he wrote short articles in various short-lived papers, it was because bright royalist students had to join battle with their republican opponents not only on the streets, but also in print.

To Drumont it seemed evident that the abandonment of the monarchist tradition and the break in the nation's continuity had effected a general confusion in which France somehow lost her true essence. Drumont's first attacks on the Republic took place years before the Dreyfus case and were directed against those who were thriving on the lay regime and its agnostic philosophy. He and other spokesmen of the Catholic-monarchist tradition looked with alarm at the industrial revolution which had established in France the rule of the financier, the banker and the industrialist. In England, as Tocqueville had remarked, the aristocracy did not consider it below their dignity to enter upon careers in industry, or to associate themselves with the emerging big entrepreneurs; in France, the traditional ruling classes meant to continue living off their large estates as absentee landlords in the glittering capital.

* *Bien-pensant* means literally "right-thinking." In French political-ideological terminology it signifies the bourgeois elements (rich peasants, shop-keepers, small town notables) and holders of socially prominent positions not only in commerce and industry but also in politics and literature.

The *bien-pensant* has a *conservative* and a *radical* variety. The conservative may be religious, but is often accused of using religion as the cloak for his attachment to his class interests and to the social order. The radical is often an agnostic; for him the achievements of the Revolution and other social conquests form a block with which he identifies his interests. For reasons different from his conservative brother's, he too is attached to the existing order of things.

What Drumont observed has been recorded in the novels of Zola. Zola furnishes acute observations about the way the scions of France's greatest families threw away their fortunes, dignity and life. While a wholesale destruction of old names and estates was going on, astute investors and capitalists (some of them with German, Spanish, and Jewish names) created and took over many leading positions in industry and banking. To a man like Drumont this situation could easily appear as a liquidation of the old, peasant and aristocratic France by busy money-grabbers with unpronounceable, barbaric names. It was, of course, a matter of opinion whether one saw in this development a sign of progress, a crisis for which the whole nation was responsible, or the conspiracy of a malevolent clique, bent on "erasing France from the map."

Drumont took the latter view. He was himself of a family of peasants and civil servants, and shared Zola's feeling concerning industrial and financial capitalism. He wanted to halt the destruction of old values, slow down the process of transition and thus save the proletariat in whom he saw not members of the International of Workers but uprooted French peasants. He rebelled against the robot mentality he saw coming and, in despair, tried to hold on indiscriminately to anything that in his tortured imagination seemed to further his cause.

In anti-Semitism Drumont found a point on which the struggle could focus. His stratagem was simple; "Drumont's anti-Semitism," wrote Bernanos, "was not a whimsical idea or an intellectual viewpoint, but a great political concept."[8] It was an attack where it was least expected and which could have become the starting point of a general offensive. This is why Drumont singled out the Jews, although the Republic, in those first decades of its stabilization, was the scene of many scandals, all of which could have served as targets.

Drumont began to preach anti-Semitism with increasing intensity. "The nation, demoralized by the Revolution," Bernanos wrote, "was in no position to resist in 1870. The active and

ambitious Jewish minority . . . became the nucleus of a new
France which nourished itself from the substance of the old . . .
Political, religious, social and family traditions were as completely emptied of their content as when the embalmers pump
the brain out through the nostrils."[9] The Jewish conquest, he
thought, was the more fatal because the Jews had been kept
away from national life for centuries, and were now allowed
to throw themselves on a society "with a broken structure, impoverished by the war." In other words, the Jews merely exploited the situation into which France had put herself; they
were, in Drumont's words, the microbes that the careless doc-
tors around France's sickbed had allowed to infest the body.

The "bearded Cassandra," as Bernanos called him, was certainly listened to, but he made no appreciable impact on the
Republic and its progress toward democratization. As political
propaganda, his words were effective but without revolutionary
significance. If the Dreyfus scandal had not arrived providen-
tially for his cause and career, Drumont would have remained
an obscure man, vituperating against all and sundry, but having
hardly any effect. The Dreyfus case provided him—and his
newspaper—with an influence in military, clerical and monarchist circles far out of proportion to the meagre political
program he is known to have had.

La Grande Peur des Bien-Pensants has to be recalled here
not only because it was first in line of the author's polemical
writings, and because—as we shall see—it marked the end of
a period in his life, but because it sheds more light on the Bernanos before World War I than on the great novelist that he
became in the decade from 1926 (the publication of *Under the
Sun of Satan*, his first novel) to 1936 (the appearance of his
last novel, *The Diary of a Country Priest*.)[10] The themes elaborated on those 450 pages appear in his youthful writings and
also in his youthful actions and attitudes. But in 1931 *La Grande
Peur* commemorated the past, rather than indicated a present
way of looking at things.

This is not to say that Bernanos had substantially changed in the interval. His fundamental attitudes always remained the same, only he possessed the great gift—quite unusual in men of his persuasion—of reinterpreting the facts in the light of experience, and the great courage to denounce former allies when the obligation of seeing the truth so dictated.* He then threw his passionate nature into the debate on the side of the newly discovered reality, but what continued to count for him were the same values he had sought before. Such a mentality is easily characterized as dogmatic, and he was the first to acknowledge it; "by the Devil," he wrote to his ex-teacher in 1906, "I shall remain dogmatic, disgusted as I am with concessions on ideas and retreats on principles. I am absolutely convinced that France's destiny depends on a traditional doctrine, the only one that suits the temperament of our race."

After the Dreyfus affair, the "intransigents" were temporarily beaten. As often happens, however, such defeats are not necessarily final; they serve, in fact, as points of departure for a new gathering of forces.

On one side, the liberal Catholics were organizing. Out of the enthusiasm of a group of young Catholics devoted to Marc Sangnier and desiring to work for the so-often postponed national and religious peace was born what was called the Sillon movement. It existed for about a decade, from the time of the Dreyfus case until its prohibition by the Vatican in 1910, and evolved towards a pure and simple socialism. Its end coincided with the reawakening of French nationalism under German threat. In the years preceding World War I, Poincaré's nation-

* "Bernanos was a man of the Right; he knew all the treasons among his friends, and precisely because they were his friends, disappointing him personally, he attacked them most violently." The pastor André Dumas, in *Cahiers du Rhône*, Essais et Témoignages, p. 166.

alism tended to rehabilitate Maurras' ideas and doom those of Sangnier. If in itself the Sillon movement proved to be a failure, its spirit penetrated Catholic consciousness and helped establish some of the first Catholic worker's unions, related youth-movements and study-groups. Sangnier's activities rendered Catholicism a "respectable" term in the context of socialist movements; they contributed to keeping alive the concept of Christian democracy, and are, in this sense, directly responsible for those post-World War II political parties and orientations which work at the reconciliation of various social doctrines and the Catholic religion.

In the first decade of the century, however, the teachings of Sangnier appeared backward to the Left, subversive to the Catholic majority and hopelessly utopian to both. They were subject to an all-round criticism, especially by Catholics who saw an extreme danger in the Sillon's identification of Christianity and democracy. Unlike the group around Maurras, they were thus taken between two fires: on the one side the men of the *Action Française* and the clergy favorable to it, and on the other side by the Radicals and Socialists who were by definition anti-clerical and agnostic and saw no place under the sun for a movement on whose banner the social question was in the uncanny neighborhood of the keys of Saint Peter. Others simply did not know what to do with Sangnier's insistence that only love, unselfishness and work for the common good would "reconcile the interests of each with the interest of the nation as a whole."

On the other hand, from 1900 on, intransigent Catholics were no longer a vague majority; their destinies, during the decades which followed the Dreyfus case, were shaped by powerful factors, and particularly by a powerful brain: that of Charles Maurras and his movement, the *Action Française*.

The mood of the French Catholics, then, in the period between the Dreyfus case and the war, was one of *dismay* before the victories of the Republic, *fear* of the Germans and of "Herr"

Jaurès' socialism and defiance of all elements they considered hostile to France: Jewish-Protestant business and banking interests, the Radical Party, Freemasons and foreigners in general. It is not surprising that Maurras and his *Action Française* (the movement and the newspaper) became the only group assertive, brilliant and aggressive enough to attract right-wing attention and adherence. And it is quite natural that the teaching of Maurras should provide the best answers to the anguished questions of old and young, priests and laymen, civilians and army-men.

NOTES

1. Albert Béguin, *Bernanos par lui-même* (Ed. du Seuil, Collection "Ecrivains de Toujours"), p. 41.
2. Quoted in *Bulletin de la Société des Amis de Bernanos*, No. 5, Christmas, 1950.
3. *Bernanos par lui-même*, No 21, p. 69.
4. *L'Imposture*, p. 214.
5. *Bulletin*, No. 1.
6. Emile Zola, *Germinal* (Fasquelle, Le Livre de poche), p. 373.
7. *Journal d'un curé de campagne*, pp. 72–3.
8. *La Grande Peur des Bien-Pensants*, p. 151.
9. *Ibid.*, pp. 136–7.
10. Two more novels appeared after this date: *Nouvelle Histoire de Mouchette* (1937) and *Monsieur Ouine* (1946), but they had been started and all but finished before 1936.

2 "Everything is a Question of Elites"

In 1906 Bernanos finished his secondary education and returned to Paris to study law. There began for him the typical student life in the capital. He was no longer a timid boy, easily persecuted by his classmates; he assumed the position of leader of his small group; "his violent sarcasm made him their mentor." Between classes at the university they attended political meetings, especially those held by their adversaries: republicans, socialists and Freemasons. They would infiltrate the groups individually before starting a well-concerted *chahut*. Or they would gather in one of the students' rooms debating long into the night, breaking up into twos and continuing the discussion while walking the deserted streets.

This way of life did not entirely satisfy them. A life of action was still preferable in their judgment to the endless debates, but it was impossible for them to satisfy this craving within the cadres of the prosperous and peaceful bourgeois republic. It is at this time that the project of emigration first occurred to Bernanos; one of his young friends, Maxence de Coleville, actually left for Paraguay. The wildness and vast spaces of South America had a great fascination for Bernanos and his friends, who "dreamed of riding half-savage horses on the pampas." (Many years later Bernanos carried out his dream.) He and his friends got involved in a strange adventure when they offered their services to the Pretender of Portugal whom they were to help back on his throne in co-operation with rebellious units of the Portuguese fleet.

ORDER: THE "CAMELOTS DU ROI"

In the next few years, Bernanos found his way. In 1908, while still a student, he signed up with the *camelots du roi*. The organization, under the auspices of the *Action Française*, was then led by Maurras' strong-arm man, Maurice Pujo, and formed a sort of shock-troop for street riots. The rank-and-file was formed by students and young working men, a sign, incidentally, that at that time, that is before the World War, the *Action Française* had not yet relinquished its popular origins and syndicalist sympathies. Naturally, however, the Catholic middle-class element predominated among the *camelots*, and this class feeling certainly contributed to the fraternal cohesion of the organization.

In 1919, in a letter to a priest friend, Dom Besse, Bernanos said that he had "joined the *Action Française* at an age when abstract ideas and strong sentiments form an explosive mixture."[1] In Maurras and his circle he recognized the elite which, he could legitimately think, would not surrender either to bribery or defeatism. He was to be most bitterly disappointed in them, as well as in the other elites in whom he placed his faith. Two years before he died he told a young visitor, a student as he had been at the time of joining the *camelots du roi*: "You see, young man, everything is a question of elites: an elite has no right to be mistaken, or it ceases to be one."[2]

Among the *camelots du roi* Bernanos was not merely an enthusiastic streetfighter. He was also to be a writer. The nocturnal debates sharpened his political views, and his reading of novels stimulated the storyteller in him. As early as 1907, when he was nineteen years old, he began to contribute short stories to *Le Panache*, an illustrated magazine of the royalist movement.

These stories have no resemblance to his later novels, and their somewhat redundant style is made even more artificial by the subjects he chose: military adventures of French history, royal battles, stories of fabulous charges, fidelity and sacrifice.

His first article of a political character he wrote in a cell of the *Santé* prison in Paris. It was shortly after he joined the *Action Française*, and he was serving a sentence after a street riot. The text appeared in *Soyons Libres*, one of those ephemeral Left Bank papers. Its title: "The Effects of the Democratic Prejudice on Literature"; below it Bernanos proudly inscribed: "written in the Santé prison."

The ideas expressed in this article follow the Maurrassian line; he attacked the romantic ideas born out of revolutionary principles as dissolvents of social relationships. They encouraged, he thought, the anarchistic tendencies latent in the individual. This is pure Maurras. But he also mentioned the isolation created by the romantic writers for themselves, isolation from society and tradition, resulting in their virtual exclusion from the national community. Along with social discipline, these writers had abandoned civilized society; they have become "barbaric nomads, hairy and famished, setting up their tents at the gates of civil society." They are not emancipated, but outlaws. In other words, inner disorder has led, in their case, to self-diminishment and narcissistic self-contemplation. Their "democratic Parnassus" had adopted the electoral procedures of democratic politics: publicity, programs, "isms," moral laxity. Instead of criticizing and correcting one another, the romantic writers exhibit their egos as the public criers their wares.

If we bear in mind that at the time of this writing nationalist youth surrounded Maurice Barrès with a veritable worship, we can understand that for Bernanos the right path for writers was the one leading back to the nation and its problems. Barrès' novels, landmarks toward national restoration (*Redressement national*), were inviting this youth not to abandon its roots in the soil and in the spirit of history. Bernanos went even further, visibly preferring the classical rigor of Maurras to the obsessed mystique of Barrès: "I give thanks to my conviction," he wrote in the same article, "for having ordered everything so well in myself that each event of my life is a station on my road toward liberty. This is the privilege of well-ordered souls . . . thanks to the mental discipline of *camelots du roi*." Order, discipline, conviction, freedom: they may sound strange coming from a twenty-one-year-old student, but they are key words for his generation.

The reason for Maurras' immense success* and deep influence on men like Bernanos is that he presented, in the teeth of many decades of Jacobin-inspired political philosophy, an extremely rich, well-thought-out, almost classically pure system, which supplied answers on the plane of theory and solutions on the level of practice. M. René Rémond writes of the *Action Française* movement that it "represented, in unequal proportions, a synthesis of all the rightist trends of the 19th century";[3] this in itself would be sufficient to explain why it attracted people of various backgrounds and opinions, and why it could afford, driven by an aggressive leader, to be less concerned with an attachment to the person of the king, than with a decisive and well-defined political choice.

But precisely because Maurras' philosophy was so strikingly coherent and forceful, it gave a general impetus and expression to other intellectual trends. In retrospect, it sometimes seems as if all lines of thought opposing the official republican-liberal ideology had emptied into the main current of the *Action*

---

* In French public life the impact of a towering personality is a greater factor than in Anglo-Saxon countries. Such a man calls forth passionate loyalties and enmities, reawakens historical precedents and embodies national and partisan ideals. He acts as a catalyst; around him political and intellectual forces crystallize their consciousness, rearrange their positions and formulate their program.

Française, which would then represent a *bloc* in the same way that the French Revolution was a *bloc*—that is, indivisible in its aspirations, achievements and program. Whatever the truth is in this respect, from the point of view of Bernanos' generation, national restoration could take only one direction, even if its battles had to be fought on several fronts: religion, Church-State relationship, the educational system and the Sorbonne-intellectuals.

THE MAURRASSIAN "BLOC"

What was the "bloc" of ideas which had such a decisive influence on Bernanos? In one sense, it is difficult to summarize the ideas of Maurras because he was not only a philosopher, a critic of society and a *littérateur*, but also a practical politician, political strategist, fearless polemicist and daily columnist for almost half a century. But behind his enormous activity there lies a unity of purpose, a Mediterranean clearness and certain unchanging principles from which everything else follows.

Against the Jacobin individualism inspired by Rousseau, Maurras put forward a concept according to which society arises not from a contract of wills, but from a fact of nature. Society, he maintained, antedates the individual, who never finds himself in isolation, but is surrounded from his birth by a family, institutions and a social structure, no matter how elementary. The individual as such is a rather weak creature, full of defects and failings; it is society that lends him strength by making him a link in the great chain of civilization. As Maurras once remarked to his friend, Henri Massis, "human weakness needs assistance from firm institutions."

The application of this political doctrine was quite obvious for Maurras at the time of the Dreyfus case. If the Jacobin doctrine of individualism were true, he wrote, we would be justified in disorganizing the army, our institutions, society itself for the sake of one individual (Captain Dreyfus); but if the State is more than the temporarily willed association of autonomous individuals, if it is a historical reality, an organism with innumerable links, then its survival and integrity constitute a more sacred cause than even that abstract justice in the name of which it is attacked and demoralized.

Monarchist and even non-monarchist nationalist opinion welcomed the views of Maurras. He explained to them that they lived in a sort of permanent illegality as long as the country was governed by the Republican regime and exposed to politicians who had their parties', not the nation's, interest at heart. As a result, they centralized the country's life in Paris so as to have everything under control, while the population had been given the doubtful benefit of voting—a mere illusion of participation in government.

Thus Maurras immediately separated what he calls the *pays réel*—the historical France, the thousand-year dynasty, regional and local government—from the *pays légal*, an artificial superstructure, alien to the nation's spirit and tradition, run by republicans, radicals and foreigners. The gap between the two could only be bridged by the return of the dynasty; the king would then resume his role as *arbitrator*, providing the unity which the parties, on account of their revolutionary origin and ideological commitments, have unscrupulously destroyed. The monarchic idea is thus deeply imbedded in the French mentality and political experience. The king is considered by many as a symbol of cohesion to which the nation may repair in times of stress and ideological dispersion. Nor is royal restoration necessarily connected with right-wing preferences; as an institution, monarchy may be a countervailing force in the interest of stability.

The idea of *unity* plays a very important role in the Maurrassian doctrine; it is not a call for governmental centralization; on the contrary, it is based on the recognition of wide regional autonomies, and on local understanding of concrete issues. Unity is rather understood as an essential function of government which must keep the conflicting interests in equilibrium. This is why Maurras emphasized the *art* and not the science of governing, a concept inspired, incidentally, by classical art and the Greek ideal of beauty.*

For Maurras, the political parties serve only disunity, corruption and selling out to the enemy, without and within. They are incapable—because of their ideology and their structure —of working for the common good. The common good is anyway incompatible with the parliamentary form of government which reduces citizen-participation to the act of casting the ballot.

The art of unity, in its political expression, demands not only the monarchy, but also a concept of distribution of power, a hierarchy as the channel for authority. The model for the best government was, for Maurras, the Catholic Church, for it is democratic at the base (parish system), aristocratic at midway (bishops and diocesan division) and monarchic at the top (Papacy). To this structure there corresponds, on the level of civilian administration in the national community, the structure of the communes, regional and corporative representation and monarchy.

This concept of authority demands a quasi-religious patriotic faith and Catholic concept of order as expressed in the writings of Saint Thomas. Maurras' thesis explicitly stated this: "All my favorite ideas," he wrote, "order, tradition, discipline, hierarchy, authority, continuity, unity, work, family, corporation, decentralization, autonomy, workingmen's organization—have been preserved and perfected by Catholicism."[4] With Maurras, French nationalism entered a new phase. A Veuillot, a Lacordaire, a Drumont belonged to the old, undisputedly Catholic France, and they fought on as many fronts as rising democracy and liberalism challenged them; in the

* In fact, the nucleus of his later expounded ideas germinated in Maurras on the occasion of a trip to Athens (1896) and a visit to the Acropolis.

Maurrassian period, nationalism—which defined itself in opposition to triumphant democracy and liberalism—began to detach itself from Catholicism as a *religion*, and to develop, instead, a *political* Catholicism. For Maurras, the Catholic Church was not principally the depository of Christ's message, a faith unquestioned and accepted without reticence; it was, rather, the only institution surviving in the modern world which was based on *hierarchy* and *order*, and which, owing to its own structure, served as a symbol and guarantee for a similarly built structure, hierarchy and order in Catholic communities and nations.*

It is on this basis that Maurras denounced the spirit of Deism: "If in the individual's conscience, which is by nature anarchic, we instill the conviction that he may establish direct contacts with the absolute Being, this idea of an invisible and faraway Master will weaken in him the respect he owes to his visible and immediate superiors. He will prefer to obey God rather than man."[5]

Throughout his life, Maurras fought the Protestant-Romantic sensibility, which favors disorder, over against the classical concept of harmony and equilibrium; he never ceased to contrast the "obscene chaos" rooted in the fuzzy soul of the Germans and British with *la belle notion du fini* represented by the Latin races. The greatest virtue of the state is stability, in the classical-Mediterranean sense of the word, that is the political approximation of the Greek esthetic ideal and the Roman genius of statecraft. The Church which preserves her visible structure against all attacks—by heretics, reformers and anticlericals—is the image of authority to be imitated by the most natural political entity, the State.

The Maurrassian line did have in its current a definite sym-

* In this respect, Maurras was the disciple of de Maistre who had written: "We may deny or venerate the ideas of religion, it makes no difference; the fact remains that these ideas are, whether true or false, the sole bases of all lasting institutions." (In *Considérations sur la France*)

pathy for socialism, and especially trade-unionism. Drumont, a master of Maurras himself, agreed with Zola, for instance, on the plight of the French proletariat, so recently of peasant stock and still attached to the peasant way of life. Before 1914 the leader of French socialism, Jean Jaurès, was hostile to Marxism.* This gave the movment a characteristic French coloration, which had a strong attraction, if not for Maurras himself, certainly for many of his followers, and nationalists outside his group—Péguy, for example. Before 1910 royalists and syndicalists had maintained a tentative peace, and only after the war did Maurras come to the definite conclusion that the Left as a whole was a danger for the nation's survival, and that trade unionism was a danger of leftist infiltration.†

By this decision, Maurras closed the door on any collaboration with the working class, and affiliated himself and his movement with bourgeois interests wherever the latter were leading him. It was a fateful decision, partly inevitable by the nature of the movement and the main trends in the 1920's. The post-Maurrassian French Right would have enormous hardships, as we shall see, in overcoming the cleavage between the working classes and the nationalists. This cleavage was to be, to a great extent, responsible for the tragedy of Vichy.

In the years preceding World War I these developments could not be foreseen. As I have said, by 1910 Maurrassism had reached a respectability that it was not to relinquish, in spite of the conflict with the Vatican in 1926, until 1945. Through

* Jaurès' rival in leadership, Jules Guesde, was, on the contrary, an orthodox Marxist. Jaurès later disappointed many of his followers by yielding to Guesde.

† "The ideas and formulas of a certain type of socialism are acceptable to Maurras within the national framework only or rather within a monarchic framework. For Maurras, the political problem cannot be solved by an economic revolution [as for the socialists and the communists] on the contrary: the economic problem will only be solved by a political revolution." Henri Massis, *Maurras et son temps*, II, p. 93.

the impact of his personality and ideas, Maurras dominated not only the discontented elements of the bourgeoisie and the Army, but also the royalist circles grouped around the Pretender and had the complete sympathy of a large section of the clergy and prelates and even of the Vatican. At first, the Pretender did not wish to involve himself with Maurras' movement, however sincerely royalist it was. The aggressiveness of the *Action Française*, its divisive effects on the nation, its all-round defiance of all whom Maurras considered enemies (including the moderates of all shades) could not be of service to a man who wished to occupy his father's throne by general consensus. Such was the power of Maurras, however, that soon he forced the moderate elements out of the royal entourage, and practically obliged the Pretender to admit publicly his debt to the movement. In 1908 *l'Action Française* became, from a bimonthly publication, a daily newspaper; and an Institute of the *Action Française* was started for the systematic teaching of royalist, Catholic and social ideas.

The Church had similar reasons to be grateful to Maurras. Leo XIII's *Rerum Novarum* was itself a sort of acknowledgment that, officially at least, Catholicism had been late in developing an awareness of the plight of the industrial proletariat and in developing instruments to prevent, or slow down, the alarming de-Christianization of the working class. On the surface, Jaurès seemed to have been justified in writing: "The Church has turned to the weak only on the day when they became strong . . . The Vatican's voice tells the people certain things only because a century ago the storm of the Revolution swept away the ancient tyrannies, and because, more recently, the fire of popular socialism has been lit on the horizon."[6]

The re-Christianization of the working class, although it shows some encouraging signs in our days, was then still only a dream. It is true, on the other hand, that not only the proletariat, but also the middle classes needed, at the time, a renewed apostolate on the part of the Church. The return to religion, if not by a majority, at least by a strong and influential minority, was achieved in no small measure, by Maurras, whose political and social analyses pointed, sometimes indirectly, to the basic truth of religion and, in particular, of Catholicism. When he wrote to the Pope in 1937, "Our political teaching has had the effect of bringing back large numbers of Protestants, free-thinkers and agnostics to the faith of the Church,"[7] he was at least partially right.

Bernanos' articles in various newspapers and magazines linked to the *Action Française* movement made him known in Maurrassian circles. When, in 1913, a vacancy occurred in the editorial position of a small weekly at Rouen, Léon Daudet, fellow-editor of the *l'Action Française* and comrade-in-arms of Maurras, recommended Bernanos as a suitable man. In October of that year, Bernanos was presented editorially to the readers of *L'Avant-Garde de Normandie:* "Monsieur Georges Bernanos," they read, "has courage and boldness in addition to his erudition."

Although he occupied this position for only six months, his Rouen experience was important. He had, by 1913, quite a reputation as a writer with a vitriolic pen and as a militant *Action Française*-man. He had tested his "boldness and courage" not only in the collective assaults on the streets and in the lecture-halls of Paris, but, alone or in the company of a few friends, at workingmen's rallies during trips in the French Northeast. Recalling their trips together in 1910, a friend reports that always and everywhere, "Bernanos was looking for *bagarre*." This is how this friend describes the setting of such an occasion: "In the large hall of the Café Napoleon, at Arras, we numbered perhaps ten among some three hundred workers, mostly socialist railway men. We occupied two tables close to a window so that we might escape if need be. Each of us had ordered half a liter of beer, served in heavy jugs which could be used as weapons if necessary."[8]

On another occasion, Bernanos and two friends went to protest against a republican priest who was saying Mass at Sains. They first attended another Mass, held in a barn by a saintly old priest sent by the bishop to counteract the other. "The Mass of M. Jouy [the priest loyal to the Republic] could not count in our eyes. So we armed ourselves for this little expedition with sticks and with a revolver. The priest and the worshippers realized that we were enemies. During his sermon, the preacher fixed us with angry eyes, Bernanos in particular, the showiest of the three musketeers. Bernanos returned his fierce look. As we were leaving, we heard some insults, but nobody dared touch us. The scandal remained of modest proportions."[9]

The articles Bernanos gave to *L'Avant-Garde* were in the line with his Maurrassian persuasion. A characteristic title from November 1913 was "French youth rallies around Maurras." The writings were filled with the usual nationalist themes, with xenophobia and anti-Semitism, defense of the monarchy and romantic effusions with regard to French soil and history. He had the distinction, while editor of *L'Avant-Garde*, to oppose Alain (Emile Chartier), the philosopher mouthpiece of French radicalism, who was professor at a Rouen lycée and a contributor to a local paper. But Bernanos had no respect for his opponent's stature and considerable political importance: the tone and style of his attacks recall Drumont's and Maurras' vituperation.

How sincere was the style Bernanos had adopted, and how deep the conviction underneath it? There are many passages in Bernanos' books and personal letters referring to his way of writing, and these passages, without exception, reveal an extreme concern with style and the usual hard labor of the authentic writer. Before any work of his was allowed to see the light of day, let alone to go to the printer, Bernanos made several drafts and innumerable corrections. Studying the latter, it is interesting to see that, as he matured, his style became increasingly simple, and whenever the first drafts are wordy, the final copy always opts for the simpler, clearer, shorter expression and for the more compact meaning. The same preoccupation is apparent in his letters, for many of which he had similarly prepared drafts and the final version of which he then recopied and placed in his meticulously kept files. His style came to reflect his personality, and convey the depth of his being. After the early period of artificiality, it always gives the impression of extraordinary directness and sincerity.

But he always wrote with great difficulty. Mauriac quotes him on the abominable misery of creating the written page: "Old chap, for the last two weeks I have been trying to catch up with lost time, to work at my new book from morning until night. But I am writing in the midst of a dense darkness; and I am less capable than ever of judging what I have produced with so much pain." And from another letter: "I sit restlessly for hours in the back of obscure cafés that I choose on purpose and where it is absolutely impossible to remain five minutes without doing something, or one drops dead from boredom. But after I have erased, torn up, recopied each sentence, and scratched them off with sand paper, I make the count only to find that I finish one and a half pages daily, on the average."

What about the conviction which underlay a sometimes artificial style? It is, of course, impossible to tell in this period how much of what Bernanos wrote was authentically his, and how much was a mere reflection of Maurras. Drumont and Maurras were certainly major influences, and we may also add Balzac for whose literary genius and social views Bernanos retained the greatest admiration.

Balzac and Drumont he admired throughout his life. The greatest compliment ever paid to him was to call him "the Balzac of ecclesiastical life." He probed the priest's soul and the priestly condition in the inexorable manner in which the author of the *Comédie humaine* studied the world of the French bourgeois, and discovered among the priests—from Donissan to Cénabre—types which had never before him appeared in our awareness, let alone in our literary heritage.

The problem of Drumont's influence on Bernanos is more difficult to ascertain. In *Les Grands Cimetières sous la lune*, in 1937, he spoke of his "thirteenth year [1901] when I read, for the first time, *France juive*, the book of my master"; but in this same book he repudiated many ideas which had been central in Drumont's works, and also in his own earlier ones, among them rabid anti-Semitism.

The third, and more decisive influence, that of Maurras, I shall discuss at length in the next chapters. We shall then have opportunities to examine the problem of how deep-rooted the Maurrassian attitude was in Bernanos—whether it was a pose, the enthusiasm of youth, a meeting of minds or something different yet.

At this point, we can see what Bernanos himself had to say, in 1931 about his pre-1914 opinions:

"When I was fifteen years old [1903], I and my friends were combatting individualism. What bad luck we had! Individualism was dead! Every nation of Europe had already, deep in its entrails, a small totalitarian state, fully formed . . . And Liberalism, oh Lord! What sticks we used to caress its backside! Alas! It no longer noticed our blows. Watched over by a few academicians in uniform, Liberalism was waiting, in a state of agony, the hour of death which the first cannon shot of the war was to announce."[10] And again: "It is true that from 1908 to 1914 I belonged to the *Camelots du roi* . . . We were not rightists, though. A circle of social studies we had founded was named *Cercle Proudhon*, a scandalous sponsorship. We were favoring nascent syndicalism. We preferred to run the risk of a workers' revolution rather than bring about a compromise between monarchy and a class [the bourgeoisie] which had remained, for a century, alien to its ancestors' tradition, to the sense of our history, and whose selfishness and greed had built a more inhuman serf system than the one our kings had long before abolished."[11]

These sentences—and many more in his later writings and speeches—do not amount, as it seems at first sight, to a repudiation of the pre-1914 attitude. They indicate rather a break with a spirit which he had thought expressed his own sentiments. "We were fighting the wrong enemy," Bernanos means to say, and he says it with his characteristic forthrightness, irony and indignation. We cannot doubt, however, that in the period in question he loyally held the ideas we outlined in this chapter, and that, at all times, he threw himself, body and soul, into battle because he followed his conscience.[12]

Even if his ideas and attitudes, in the years preceding World War I, were not so much his as those of his milieu, we can detect Bernanos' deep originality in his patriotism and religious fervor. Love of France was, at the time, an exacerbated emotion. Everyone's passion had been stirred up by the Dreyfus case, considered, in a sense, the continuation of the 1870 defeat, and a defeat in its own right. The novelists Maurice Barrès and Paul Bourget, the critics Brunetière and Lemaître, Péguy and Maurras in their own very different ways, were all celebrating the cult of France. But there is a tone of unvarnished love of the homeland when Bernanos speaks of *la patrie*, a love which finds the same expressions of despair as that of a young man wanting to be ever closer to his beloved. "I am made of a coarse material," he wrote in *Les Enfants humiliés* (1940), "I am as faithful to my country as only animals and trees can be." And again: "Nothing will ever make of me an uprooted man, I could not live five minutes with my roots torn out of the soil; only death will achieve this. As long as I live I shall belong to my land as I belong to my childhood."[13]

To speak of Bernanos' religious fervor is to speak of the whole man, since the quality and intensity of his faith permeated his whole being. Hans Urs von Balthasar's long book is devoted to a study of the Christianity of Bernanos, and its most important lesson is that religion is the one key to every one of his thoughts and actions. Again, as in the case of his patriotism, at first glance it might be difficult to discover the originality of his religious faith in a period when nineteenth-century materialism began to give way to a religious renaissance among writers, poets and philosophers. The influence of Bloy and Bergson, to mention two very different sources, occasioned a number of spectacular conversions, and the Dreyfus case itself led many a man of letters into the Catholic camp. "Huysmans, Claudel, Bourget, Brunetière became converted and gave their reasons, with Barrès, that 'sound laws for the individual, as well as for society are in harmony with the Ten Commandments.' Jammes, Psichari, Massis, Maritain longed for a meaning in life which the mechanical conception of the world denied them."[14]

Brunetière followed the same thinking: "In order to combat dilettantism, individualism, anti-nationalism, I have been seeking a stable point; after having looked in vain for such a point in the lessons of science and of philosophy, I have found it and found it only in Catholicism."[15] As these words indicate, the starting point of many of these conversions was intellectual, *often political*. Despair and disgust over the conquest of materialism, incompetence,* the "Jewish mentality," and Freemasonry prompted at least the first step toward Catholicism of many good minds.

But again, with Bernanos it was different. He was a Catholic and he could not imagine himself as anything but a Catholic. When, in 1926, at the time of the appearance of *Under the Sun of Satan*, his publisher asked him to fill out a form with his personal data, he put down with smiling irony: "Catholic since birth, not even a convert."

* Emile Faguet, for example, devoted a book to democracy "the cult of incompetence."

Bernanos was as unable to think of himself detached from the Church as detached from France. He reminds the reader in many moving passages that although he often violently criticizes the earthly representatives of the Church, he would not hesitate to beg for forgiveness, in the penitent's shirt, if he were cast out from among the faithful. He breathed only within Catholicism, and if he chose Brazil as his place of voluntary exile after the Munich humiliation, it was to be surrounded by the well-known climate which only a tradition of Catholicism can create.

This intimacy with the life of faith and religion explains why he was so much at home with priests, churches and liturgy. When he attacked the Church, its institutions and personnel, he did so with the naturalness of one who inhabits the house, not as a timid outsider. He was able to drive away from his sick-bed (it became his death-bed) a priest-professor of canon law because he disliked the pedantic mentality, the professional attitude; but he welcomed, humbly and in the spirit of the child, the abbé Pézeril who came to administer the last rites. Never a pose, never a mask, as von Balthasar remarks, "Bernanos gave the perfect example of lay priesthood."[16]

NOTES

1. *Bulletin*, No. 11, July 1952.
2. Reminiscences of André Laugier in *Cahiers du Rhône, Essais et témoinages* (Ed. du Seuil, 1949).
3. René Remond, *La Droite en France* (Aubier, 1954), p. 178.
4. Quoted by Jacques Juilliard, "La Politique religieuse de Ch. Maurras," *Esprit*, March 1958.
5. Note II for *Trois Idées politiques*, in Charles Maurras, *Oeuvres Choisies*, II, p. 88.
6. Quoted by Marcelle Auclair, *La Vie de Jaurès* (Ed. du Seuil, 1954), p. 193.

7. Father Clerissac, a priest with a great influence on intellectuals like Maritain, Massis, and Maurras himself, believed that the restoration of the King and of religion must go hand in hand. He saw whence were coming the blows against the concepts of hierarchy and order, essential to the life of the Church. This is why he detested, as M. Maritain records, democracy as the source of evil. Like so many other priests, he favored the *Action Française* because it fought anti-intellectualism at the Sorbonne and elsewhere.

8. Henri Tilliette, "Bernanos en Artois," *Bulletin*, No. 14, February 1953.

9. *Ibid.*

10. *Les grands Cimetières sous la lune*, p. 70.

11. *Ibid.*, p. 48.

12. "The surest means to be unlike anybody is to be naively what one is, to say naively what one thinks." *Le Crépuscule des vieux*, p. 25.

13. Pp. 36–7.

14. Adrien Dansette, *Histoire religieuse de la France contemporaine* (Flammarion, 1951), Vol. II.

15. Quoted in *Ibid.*, p. 478.

16. Hans Urs von Balthasar, *Le Chrétien Bernanos* (Ed. du Seuil, 1956), p. 124.

3 *"The New Treason"*

BERNANOS was twenty-six years old when the first World War broke out. It was said of his generation that it entered the war with white kid gloves on, as an affair of honor for young Christian knights. If that was the attitude at the beginning, it soon changed; the battle of the Marne, the alarm in Paris that the early defeat of 1870 might repeat itself, and then the settling down to a hopeless, unknightly trench warfare in the muddy fields of Flanders gave an altogether different image of modern military conflicts.

The first months of the war saw the names of some very gifted writers on the casualty list: Alain-Fournier, the author of *Le Grand Meaulnes*, Ernest Psichari, Renan's nephew, and Charles Péguy, who shed his blood on the battlefields he had celebrated in his invocations to France, her cathedrals and heroes.

Captain, now Lieutenant-Colonel Dreyfus, was also fighting in the ranks of the French army. The army, essentially untouched in its morale by the great scandal and the personnel shake-up which followed it, was now the symbol of national reconciliation, with one sacred duty: to drive the enemy off the French soil, to avenge the humiliation suffered almost half a century before. The *"union sacrée"* was a real achievement, even if the assassination of Jaurès on the eve of the war had not presaged a smooth functioning for it. In fact, the army was not above the hope of taking things into its hands once the conduct of the war officially facilitated such an evolution. Some generals, and civilians behind them, were not convinced that the socialists in the Cabinet, among whom was Prime Minister René Viviani and the orthodox Marxist, Jules Guesde, could be trusted; both the French and the German Socialist parties had tried, during the summer of 1914, to come to a peaceful agreement above the heads of their respective governments and vote against the military budgets. As early as December 30, 1914, Abel Ferry, a member of the Cabinet doing his military service on the front, remarked in his *Carnets de Guerre:* "The generals are fulminating against the civilians. They are now the masters in all of France. The Prefects no longer exist, the deputies are browbeaten. There is much bungling in all this, but some of it is intentional and shows the reactionary-clericalism has put on the military uniform in order better to fight— the Republic."

For the simple front-line soldier this hidden conflict between the two traditional camps (a conflict more or less alive until it was crushed by the strong fist of Clemenceau) was at best unreal. As Bernanos was to write afterwards, for them anything that was going on "back home" was "Behind"; they complained about its carefree life while they fought an enemy made invisible by the heavy rain, and they loved its comfort, and pleasures on their furloughs. Bernanos himself, at this time engaged to the young Rouennaise, was a serious soldier, fighting the war and winning citations and, in the long lulls between battles, reading and writing a great deal, sometimes sitting on a trench parapet, exposed to enemy gunfire. His comrades knew him as a man of great courage, but also as a fierce and fiery disputant, who, between his books and his favorite discussion topics, seemed to fight a war of his own.

Many books—histories, memoirs, novels, manifestoes—have been written about the great disillusionment that followed the war. "Every twenty years," Bernanos wrote later, "the youth of the world asks a question to which society cannot give an answer. For lack of an answer, it mobilizes."[1] The returning soldiers, as always happens, were shocked by the effrontery of those who seemed to have profited by their suffering and sacrifice. Victory was "stolen" from them, and the thieves were the "bourgeois," the "socialists" or simply, as Bernanos liked to call them, the "imbeciles." They were painfully aware of disappointment after the pre-war idealism as they entered an era promising no heroism and no distinction. What had they been fighting for? "Those who did not live then," Bernanos recalled twenty-five years later, "cannot know what disgust is . . . I was walking the boulevards, tossed between contentment and misery, but always with that empty feeling of anxiety in my stomach. . . . Everywhere, on the streets, on the terraces of cafés, in front of factories and workshops, I saw the men who, for five years, had been my equals, my comrades . . . The army had proceeded to demobilize them as if they had been hand grenades to be stored on shelves . . . But it was unnecessary to treat them like explosives . . . The war had not turned them into rebels, not even into adventurers."[2]

To Bernanos, Paris and France appeared in those first post-war months as a "world fair" where the "international rabble" gathered to celebrate a victory which did not belong to them, to which they were not entitled. "The temperature was that of a bordello, the franc fallen below zero, and the newspaper editors, made hysterical by their own publicity, were discovering a genius every day. . . . On the boulevards one could sense the smell of the extermination camps which were to open twenty years later . . . My comrades and I must have been the last of scoundrels for having tolerated that from the war France should fall directly into a carnival."[3]

For the time being, the only answer to every question was victory won. The old radical Clemenceau shared the acclamations with marshals Foch and Joffre. In their person, the *union sacrée* continued, although the government of the *Bloc national* was right-wing. Maurras himself ordered his forces to participate actively in political life. Was this a new treason? Bernanos asked himself. Would Maurras come to terms with the Republic? Would the right-thinking bourgeoisie whom he represented forget the King and choose prosperity instead? "We (young royalists) knew that the bourgeoisie had always sacrificed the monarchy to its own greed, to its vanity, to a kind of conservatism that it takes for tradition . . . We knew well that the bourgeoisie had always interposed itself between the Nation and the King."[4] For these reasons, Bernanos left the *Action Française* movement in 1920. In *Nous autres, Français*, he tells us that Dom Besse approved of his step.

These were difficult years for Bernanos and his growing family. After some fruitless attempts at finding a position, he finally accepted one as an inspector for an insurance company and began a life not in any way different from that of a traveling salesman. The one redeeming factor was his unceasing trust that one day his literary efforts might be crowned with success. In the meantime, however, he needed all his faith and energy to continue. His situation was unhappy. He liked the cheerful side of life, was fond of horses, hunting and weapons, good food and wine; he was, in the description of a friend, handsome, well-dressed, very much alive, a brilliant conversationalist, a man admired and loved by those around him. But his family responsibilities imposed on him years of miserable travel in those villages and small towns of the Northeast which he later described so vividly in his novels.

He was still carrying in his head the unborn characters of those novels. Their birth cost him immense pain. "I am no writer," he noted later: "The mere sight of a sheet of white paper is a torture to my soul. The physical concentration that writing demands is so odious to me that I avoid it as far as possible. I am writing in cafés at the risk of being taken for a drunkard, which I would perhaps become if the Republic did not levy such high taxes on the comforting alcohol. Instead of these drinks, I swallow, all through the day, innumerable cups of sweetish café-crème, with a fly inside. I write on the tables of cafés because I could not do for a long stretch of time without human faces and voices around me."[5]

In 1926 he published his first novel, *Sous le Soleil de Satan* (*Under the Sun of Satan*). It was a literary event on several accounts. In spite of the conversion of many writers of his and the previous generation, Catholics had still been waiting for the Catholic novelist who would renew both the religious and the literary inspiration in France. The novels of a Paul Bourget were stilted and pedantic; in them religion was confused with the religious issue, with middle-class conservatism, and with attacks on official Sorbonne philosophy. Two promising writers, Psichari and Alain-Fournier, were dead. Mauriac was thought by many to be disturbingly soft towards the sin of the flesh, so that Maritain even warned him not to connive with his sex-tormented heroines. And the non-Catholics had Proust to inscribe on their honor roll.

Léon Daudet, Maurras' fellow-editor and a member of the Goncourt Academy, claimed in April 1926: "Besides Proust Bernanos is the genuinely new writer of the post-war generation." French Catholics would no longer have to scan the horizon anxiously for their novelist. They would have him in the person of Bernanos. Daudet put him on the same plane with Balzac and Barbey d'Aurevilly (both immensely admired by Bernanos) and exclaimed: "People were asking: Who will be *the* post-war novelist? Very well, here he is. Bernanos announces a new form, a new orientation of the French and Latin mind."[6]

The other order of importance of *Sous le Soleil de Satan* was political. Asked by an interviewer why he had written his novel, Bernanos explained that it was an act of defiance: the war had caused his generation to despise a State which imposed false slogans and sentiments. Some one had to stand up and become the witness. "I threw a saint (the abbé Donissan) in the path of the idiotic jubilation and the slogans of victory."*

Sous le Soleil de Satan was, in a sense, a *succès de scandale;* not for the usual reason, that is, for pointing, through fictitious characters, to real people, but because it drove very far and very deep the analysis of passions, sin and evil. (The greatest scandal of all was provoked by the figure of the Devil whom Donissan actually meets one night as he passes across the fields. Speaking of the Devil to a generation of cynics could only have provoked belittling smiles except that everybody felt the profound convictions behind it, born from an absolute faith.) The tone of the book was such that the interviewer asked Bernanos if he had given up hope. "No," answered Bernanos, "my hope is in the Kingdom of God. Here on earth the present civilization is betting on man's lower half. We, on the contrary, wager on the other; we believe that the world will be saved by heroism or by nothing at all."†

It is a reply that reflects the general tone of the post-war period: the deep dissatisfaction with the way things were going, the dissatisfaction which underlay the political movements on the surface. The voice of Bernanos sounded, of course, more dramatic than other voices; but, as often in his later career, he found in a fictional character—this time in the figure of Donissan, then in Mouchette, Cénabre, Chantal, M. Ouine—the point

---

* "Disillusionment with the men of 1920," he wrote, "drove me to write *Sous le Soleil de Satan* much the same way as the abbé de Rancé decided to enter the Trappist order when he saw his mistress' face with maggots swarming on it and her blond hair glued to her forehead by the froth of decomposition." *La France contre les Robots*, p. 112.

† Bernanos was himself, at the time, a kind of hero in the eyes of many young Catholics who were disconcerted by recent events. As Jean de Fabrègues wrote of him, he had given them a position, a direction in life; "This is what we were seeking, crushed and torn as we were between nothingness and infinity." (In *Réaction*, May, 1931).

of gravity of a malaise, seemingly exaggerated at the time but becoming, with every passing year, more real, and more representative of the general climate of opinion, sentiments and attitudes. With his artistic intuition he dug deeper than would those who habitually skim the surface of national life; what he called "the analysis of passions" displayed, in fact, a handful of incredible dirt—evil almost literally alive and squirming, which was to grow and cover the land.

The Right, especially, had grave reasons to be bitter. In 1924 the so-called *Cartel des gauches* (or Leftist coalition) of radicals and socialists defeated the *Bloc national;* Herriot and Léon Blum became leading figures of the Republic. A strong minority had already seceded from the Socialist Party and formed the Communist Party, attracted, naturally, to Soviet Russia. Communism was an exasperating political phenomenon for the conservative middle classes and for the clergy, because it gave shelter to an already de-Christianized working class and an important platform to left-wing intellectuals.

The right-wing youth who had returned so disappointed from the war would not necessarily have rejected the Communist Party. Many of them willingly joined the socialists, whose patriotism was no longer questioned, because disgust with the "System" was uppermost in their minds, and only a revolutionary movement was able to answer their needs. The personal case-histories of many right-wing and even Fascist leaders of the years 1934–1944 lead through socialist and communist party-membership. Those who later left these parties and became violent enemies of the Left did so for one main reason: they had come to the conclusion that Marxism, while valid in its criticism, much of its economic analysis and some of the remedies offered, remains blind to the values of family, nation, tradition and religion (in what may be called its Maurrassian interpretation). In this way, the "national" was opposed by them to the "social," or, rather, the two were combined, waiting for the day when a powerful mind might bring them into a synthesis.

Such a mind remained obstinately absent—on French soil, at least. But the great illusion of this generation, a generation of well-brought-up, tradition-respecting, young and brilliant men, was to believe that Charles Maurras incarnated it. Maurras, however, incarnated many things to many people; first of all, as we have seen, he was the standard bearer of the integrist clergy, the aristocracy, the high bourgeoisie, whose interests were insufficiently protected by the conservative politicians, and the predominantly Catholic lower middle classes. After the war, the *Action Française*, eager to play an active role, became wedded to these classes and interests, all of them worshipping the status quo and afraid of unrest in the streets and factories. Younger men like Bernanos and Drieu La Rochelle were thus caught between the Marxism of the Left, which they rejected, and the conservatism of their own milieu, which disgusted them. Various people solved this dilemma in various ways. Drieu, for example, chose Fascism and was to end in complete despair; Simone de Beauvoir, also from a *bien-pensant* family, abandoned the ideals of her class and became a "progressive"; Thierry Maulnier was brought back to moderation by the war; finally, Bernanos was to be saved by his inalterable faith from what André Rousseaux called "the temptation of despair."

In the 1920's these particular paths were by no means clear. The patriotism of young intellectuals found, almost automatically, the Maurrassian channels which satisfied their antipathies and articulated their oppositions. "In order to appear up-to-date," M. Yves Simon writes of this period, "you had to denounce liberal errors, scoff at liberty, equality and fraternity, joke about progress, look skeptical when human dignity and the rights of conscience were spoken of, affirm authoritatively that every plan for international order was a bloody dream, and sneer at the League of Nations."[7]

Long forgotten were the days when, learning about the new newspaper, Maurice Barrès had exclaimed with contempt: "What an absurd enterprise! The annoying thing is that they claim parentage with my ideas. I fear they will compromise me . . . Well, at any rate, they won't last six months!"[8] Now, after the war, it was very different. The newspaper had become an aggressive, brilliant sheet, which gave morning comfort to the worried citizen cursing the Republic while eating his breakfast and preparing to leave for work. It was also a "personalized" paper; it made the reader participate in the personal political campaigns, attacks and vicissitudes of the editors, so that they might feel even more incensed by injustices which were committed against them too. The articles—signed Maurras, Daudet, Bainville—were brilliantly and authoritatively written political analyses: trenchant, lucid, on a prophetic tone when necessary and liberally interspersed with invectives. On the masthead the paper bore the inscription: *Organe du nationalisme integral*, thereby reducing to size or altogether belittling whoever else claimed to be a patriot. Inside, there was a list of hotels in Paris and in provincial towns which subscribed to *l'Action Française*. This was not only a form of advertisement; it further strengthened the reader's feeling that he was part of a family, of a network which covered the whole country.

In 1926, in the climate of Maurrassian influence and successes, there suddenly broke the news of the Vatican condemnation forbidding Catholics membership in the movement and the reading of the paper. The works of Maurras, found contradictory to Catholic teaching, had been on the Index since 1914; this time, this fact was given publicity, and Maurras and Daudet were designated by name as the authors of articles "which every sensible man must recognize as being written against the Apostolic See and the Pope himself." The measures were just as unequivocal: ecclesiastics absolving the faithful for reading and favoring the *Action Française* were to be deprived of the right to hear confession; seminarians found to be attracted to it, discharged as unfit for the priestly vocation; the faithful continuing to read and accept the ideas of Maurras, considered public sinners and as such deprived of the sacraments.

The Church (and Pius XI) decided to follow this path for two main reasons. First, the ideas of Maurras concerning religion, Catholicism and the Church were shaped, as we have seen, by his deep conviction that beliefs and the institutional channels by which they are expressed are important mainly for their *political* influence. In this sense, his admiration for the Catholic Church was addressed not so much to the bearer of Christ's *message*, but rather to the splendid *organization* which had transmitted the ideal of the Roman state to the barbarian nations of the Middle Ages and made of them civilized communities and well-ordered societies. While he spoke of the evangelists as "four shabby Jews," he celebrated the pagan Greek and Roman element in the Church. His preference for the *political* made him discard the essence of the Christian message—to him it was a Levantine-Jewish concoction surviving in Protestantism—and retain the hierarchical structure which Christianity had adopted from the pagan state. As Vialatoux wrote in 1927, Maurras did not suggest that the Church ought to be paganized; rather it was his view that the Church actually had a pagan spirit and structure. In fact, this was her merit in his eyes and the reason why he saw no need to assign a new mission to the Church. He merely recognized her traditional mission.

The second, less apparent reason for the Vatican's break with the *Action Française* could be found in the socio-political situation of post-war France. We have seen that it was largely under the threat of socialist successes at the end of the nineteenth century (in Italy as well as in France) that Pope Leo XIII had persuaded the leaders of French Catholicism to work out a modus vivendi with the Republic. A similar threat and one of more serious proportions was now becoming increasingly evident; the Communist Party and, in general, the repeated electoral victories of the Left had to be interpreted as ominous signs. The second success of the *Cartel des gauches* in 1927 confirmed the warning of Archbishop Dubois of Paris that the working classes had reached a danger point in their process of de-Christianization. If the trend was to be stopped, the Church of France had first to dissociate herself from the *Action Française*, now identified with conservative-bourgeois interests. And she had to do it fast and with one stroke since many integrist (monarchist) bishops, not to mention the lower clergy, had been encouraging Maurras in his intransigent position. The decision, in order for it to be unquestioned, had to come from the top.

The effect of this decision was far-reaching, and more disastrous perhaps, in view of the easily identifiable line which leads from the events of 1926 to 1940 and to Vichy, than the Dreyfus scandal a generation earlier. The camp of Catholic intellectuals was gravely divided over the issue; the majority submitted to the Church (Maritain, for example), and a minority remained loyal to Maurras (Massis, for example). Both sides were to carry the scars of broken friendships and the burden of a new political isolation. Thus the Vatican decision, beside being a matter of conscience, was also a step with important political consequences. It aggravated the spiritual-political crisis of right-wing youth by dividing it just at the moment when the Left was accumulating its victories. The defeat of the *Action Française*, a defeat administered by the Church and therefore creating even more confusion in less subtle minds, caused these young men to join new, extremist groups and leagues and give up hope for an orderly, parliamentary opposition to the regime. The immediate consequence of leftist victory in the 1927 elections was the emergence of small, right-wing groups like "Jeunesses Patriotes," "Faisceau," etc., which were to take the Maurrassian succession; outwardly different, they were all, as M. René Rémond writes, expressions of the old rightist "dream to satisfy the proletariat and to reassure, at the same time, the possessing classes."[9]

What was Bernanos' attitude during a period which affected so many of the young men of his generation?

His main, absorbing interest was still, of course, in literature and in the characters who now began to step out of his imagination to create a magnificent new world of fiction. But there was always a close relationship in his mind between this fictional world and that of reality including his country's political situation. At any event, the writing of several novels, which established him firmly in the eyes of the critics and the public, did not absorb all his energies; the political issues continued to preoccupy him, and between his experiences and their artistic distillation in the novels, he slowly emerged as an unparalleled diagnostician of his time and of the evils which were gnawing at it. In short, he assumed, consciously or unconsciously, the role of Drumont as a critic of society, the relentless prober of its rotted parts and a herald of its moral regeneration.

His departure from the *Action Française* brought no ill-feelings on either side; otherwise, considering how rancorous the editors were, Daudet would perhaps not have praised Bernanos' first novel. Yet, Bernanos had few illusions left concerning the chances of his country's restoration through adherence to the Maurrassian ideals. We have seen that he understood the new orientation of the movement: its submission to the interests of the conservative bourgeoisie, instead of becoming the elite Bernanos had expected. As he wrote some twenty years later, the *Action Française* had been founded half a century before "as a reaction against the spirit and the methods of the bourgeois world; since then it has slowly adapted itself to the image of the same people whom it had fought most brutally."[10] In other words, in Bernanos' estimation, the followers of Maurras ceased to be an elite. This was so for an even more important reason than the treason of having allowed themselves to be pushed into the enemy camp. The evil lay deeper; it was to cost Bernanos a great deal to probe the spirit of Maurrassism and to reveal the psychology of Maurras himself. We shall see, in fact, that beyond his polemical writings against Maurrassian philosophy, his novels too are obsessed by the figure of the potentially great soul (that is, Maurras) gone wrong, dried up, detached from living faith and charity. But at this point we are at the beginning of this great discovery, when Bernanos felt that the failure of the *Action Française* was due to the lack of a true Christian faith in its leaders and in the unholy alliances that their essential opportunism necessarily brought about. Bernanos was forced to conclude that, no matter how violent and authoritative, Maurras lacked the one characteristic trait of the elite-man, that of "taking risks, the risk of thinking and acting." Maurras was a leader because he could take for granted a large camp of followers, many of whom misunderstood him, some of whom, as events were to prove, were ready to use him. This was not the "leader" as Bernanos meant it. He began to look at Maurras not as a great man (he never stopped admiring him as a writer), but as a social and political phenomenon, a product of the conservative bourgeoisie and the clerical mentality.

THE BOURGEOIS PROLETARIAT

It is important to understand Bernanos' analysis of the French middle classes, deprived of an elite and also of roots in a world of increasing social mobility. He compares them to seaweeds which, when detached from the rocks that saw them born, begin to agitate in the currents until they end by rotting away in some stale water. "The abdication of the real elite has cleared the way for a *bourgeois proletariat* which now faces the workers' proletariat. It lacks, however, the stability of the old middle class, the latter's family traditions and commercial honesty. The hazards of economic anarchy throw up new layers upon new layers." Instead of exercising a respectable activity, handed down from father to son, the *commerçant* becomes one by taking advantage of France's overburdened system of merchandise distribution and by increasing the number of intermediaries between producer and retailer.

In the eyes of Bernanos, these new *commerçants* were simple, unimaginative profiteers, leading a despicable existence and despising the classes whose parasites they were. "They owe everything to the moral, mental and social anarchy of the last century, to the decadence of the elites, to the enslavement of the individual worker. They know that if a more humane regime succeeded in reincorporating the latter into the nation, the absurd prestige of small-scale commerce would soon become nothing but a bad dream . . . Those of us who have had a chance to talk with skilled workers know that they have the empirical knowledge equivalent to that of an engineer. Do you not find it ignoble, then, that the first-comer, just because he can pay cash and make an undue profit on the merchandise, should feel his social superior? . . . This bourgeois proletariat has neither tradition, nor principles, but it has sure instincts. This instinct tells them that any serious social reform would return them to a state of nothingness. Yet, the men on the Right, nationalists and clericalists, think that it might be smart to enroll these people *en masse* into the middle classes where they would form the footsoldiers in the great war for the social status quo."[11]

"I do not believe," Gaëtan Picon writes of Bernanos' social criticism, "that it is possible to apply the principles of Marxist critique to the political thinking of Bernanos. . . . It is true, however, that he puts the bourgeoisie on trial in all his works; no class-inspired ideology underlies his thought." And he quotes the following lines from *Lettre aux Anglais:* "It is obviously regrettable that our workers let the Marxist lawyers plead the case of their revendications. But if they had waited for the Jesuits to do it, what would they have obtained in the past fifty years? When, before 1888, the government had not yet recognized their right of association, where were then the Reverend Jesuit Fathers?"[12] We have seen that Jaurès had the same thing to say.

Again and again Bernanos indicts the cadre of the bourgeoisie—the right-wing nationalists and the clericalists—for failing in their task, for being self-appointed leaders of society and for alienating the masses of French people by their pursuit of selfish interests. He points to the insane fear the bourgeoisie and its Maurrassian defenders have of the working class, a fear which turns into fury and hatred, and which explains, ultimately, why no protector could be considered strong enough in the long run.

Bernanos was never attracted, however, by either socialism or that strange mixture which, in Germany, was called National Socialism and which in France finally found expression in the *révolution nationale* under Vichy. On the contrary, he never ceased to expect the coming of a new elite to take the organic succession of the old aristocracy. Its virtues, rooted in the soil, would restore *le petit peuple* to their rightful position. He obstinately believed in the existence of the "real" French people and of a vast undercurrent of sober opinion, the threads of which could be pulled together only by a king.

"There is a bourgeoisie of the Left and a bourgeoisie of the Right; but the nation is neither leftist nor rightist: it is one. These labels are profitable to the demagogue only, because they create currents and counter-currents which he knows how to manipulate. The idea I have of the people is not inspired by any democratic sentiment. Democracy is an invention of intellectuals, the same way as the monarchy of M. de Maistre. Monarchy, after all, cannot live on theses and antitheses; . . . it never has the time to define the nation, it takes it as it is. . . . The notaries and lawyers who made the Revolution of 1789 thought they could put aside the people, govern without them.

'First we must build an elite,' they said. . . . So in the new building, constructed according to the lofty Roman architecture, there was no room for the people of France. This is not surprising; the liberal architect did not any more concern himself with lodging his proletariat than the Roman architect with lodging his slaves. But while the slaves were a horde of Helots, a sacrificed and corrupt human cattle, modern society exposes to destruction an admirable creation of nature and history. . . . our old and proud people."[13]

THE WORKER ELITE

For Bernanos, this old and proud people is often the proletariat. This had once been the idea of Maurras himself. As M. Léon Roudiez remarks, in his youth Maurras would have welcomed "reforms inspired by the scientific spirit of a Taine and a Zola; he even favored associations of workers and employers which would have opened, for the more intelligent elements of the working class, a field of constructive action instead of one of instigation for strikes."[14] Bernanos accused Maurras precisely for having abandoned the proletariat and sacrificed it to his concept of order; he felt that Maurras respected what was "respectable," that is "useful." He did not attack injustice and lie, but the revolt that injustice and lie call forth. What was particularly abhorrent to Bernanos in Maurras' thought was the attitude implicit in a short social parable, *Les Serviteurs*, which Maurras wrote before the war. In it the god Mercury announces to Crito, Socrates' rich and noble friend who is now in the Elysian fields, that Christ has arrived for the liberation of slaves. When Crito's own slaves hear the "good news" they throw themselves at their master's feet, imploring him not to set them free but to keep them in his service and under his protection.

Bernanos understood what is profoundly immoral in this paternalistic approach, and impractical in it in the modern world which simply does not accept such an attitude. For there was in this attitude a certain rancor *vis-à-vis* the working class (Crito's slaves) for not conforming to the place and role assigned to them, for not submitting, spontaneously, to what Maurras, speaking for their masters, defined as the best of possible worlds. Bernanos understood and (in *Lettre aux Anglais*) vehemently denounced this absurd and grotesque desire of the conservative nationalists not only to impose their rule, but to have it accepted cheerfully—an attitude of detesting a France which refused to love them.

Bernanos' own way of looking at the proletarian problem is best expressed in a lecture on the Commune of 1871 which he gave at the *Institut d'Action Française* in March 1930.

He had chosen to speak on the Commune because of the similarity he saw between that period of crisis and the political climate around 1930. In the 1870's the radicals and conservatives had joined forces to crush the people and with the people the genuinely French socialist tradition. Bernanos was fearful that the same kind of coalition would operate against the working classes in his own time. He spoke of the nineteenth-century remnants of the guild system which, by the end of the Old Regime, had gotten rid of its servitudes and had produced an individualistic class of workers, many of whom were deeply religious and often royalist. This typically French socialist tradition, which was fighting the capitalist enslavement brought upon it by the descendants of the enriched Jacobin bourgeoisie, survived till the end of the Second Empire around 1870.

It was at this point that the greatest injustice was perpetrated on the popular forces. The government of Thiers had refused to call together the Chambers since it was not strong enough to face the deputies' questions and opposition. Instead, it retired to Versailles and stood by while the Prussians invaded the capital and indirectly caused the insurrection. As if the first treason of delivering to the Prussians the road to Paris had not been enough, the little people and the workers of Paris were then betrayed a second time; the Versailles government ordered a ruthless repression, the joint work of ex-Radical turncoats and conservative politicians and generals.

Of the two Bernanos singled out the conservatives for his special anger. The conservatives, he told his audience, prevented national reconciliation as they had done before and were to do again. In fact, this is why they were "imbeciles" (Bernanos' favorite apostrophe for Machiavellians who turn out to be dupes), since they missed every opportunity to deserve the nation's acclaim, to become its elite. In the tragic spring of 1871 they ought to have gone to the people and used a language that all would have understood. Instead they turned on the people.

Bernanos thus looked at the Parisian Commune as an event explicable by the absence of dialogue between two sections of the nation. His analysis remains on the level of nationalism and patriotism, while the classic study of the same events by Marx goes deeper and explores the economic background of the war, of the insurrection and its failure. But, in a sense, Bernanos' way of looking at 1871 encompasses the economic issues as well since he never forgets to locate the responsibility of an enriched bourgeois class determined to protect its economic interests through war, repression and regimes built on injustice.

Yet this was not socialism, but an understanding of the urgent need to close the widening gap between the working class and the nation. Naturally, the political parties advocated just this; but, in Bernanos' estimation, they used the workers as an instrument for vote-gathering, and their union, the powerful *Confédération Générale du Travail*, as a road to power. He believed, on the contrary, in a movement generated within the working class, helped and encouraged by the non-political forces of the nation, by elites such as he expected the royalists to be.

A few years later he came to the conclusion that, since all the potential elites failed one after the other, "the worker elite is the only aristocracy that was left, the only elite that the bourgeoisie of the nineteenth and twentieth century has not managed to debase."[15]

The concept of a "worker elite" is, under the conditions created by contemporary economic developments, certainly not more vague than the concept of the "working class," which repelled Bernanos with its collectivistic and deterministic ring. On this point, his thought was in harmony with that of Drumont and Sorel, the early Maurras, and, among the younger thinkers, Gustave Thibon and Simone Weil. All believed in some form of de-politization of the workers, although some stressed their re-Christianization, others their finding of new roots. All agreed, as Simone Weil expressed so eloquently, that the workers need protection not only against capitalist exploitation, but also against the various forms of power which a democracy develops as inevitably as more brutal regimes. "Our age," she wrote, "has for its mission, for its vocation, the establishment of a civilization based on the spirituality of work. It would be desirable that all those circles in which traces of sober thinking still survive, participate in this task: the Churches, labor unions, literary and scientific groups."[16]

It is evident that Bernanos had, in these years, increasingly grave apprehensions that the *Action Française* was going to betray the country in the same way that Thiers and the Bonapartist generals had betrayed it in 1871. It seemed that opportunism and Machiavellian tactics prevented the Maurrassian intelligentsia from facing up to the issues of the modern world and placing the good of the nation above ephemeral partisan interests. "Nothing will prevent me," he was to write in *Lettres aux Anglais*, "from denouncing the fatal break which came to separate, after 1918, the nation from its elites. The crime that this break represents cannot be attributed to the nation. I accuse the French elites of having betrayed the people. . . . Since 1925 [the year after the first leftist electoral victories] the elites have taken, vis-à-vis the rest of the nation, an attitude of perpetual censorship, of sly defeatism, not to say of cynical contempt."[17]

The remedy he offers is loyalty to the monarchist tradition because the king alone could maintain the balance between conflicting groups, and he alone could remind the elite of their duties. A modern prince, he thought, would probably find it easier to treat with the leadership of the proletariat than with business corporations and banks." The fatal blindness of the nationalists, in Bernanos' judgment, was to relinquish gradually their loyalty to king and tradition and to imagine that by seeking alliance with the "banks and corporations," they could indefinitely postpone a new insurrection.

It is characteristic of what one could call the "prophetism" of Bernanos that he feared that this insurrection might become the greatest national catastrophe since the Revolution. He seemed to think that while the *bien-pensants* of the nineteenth century were still permeated with tradition, the conservatives of the twentieth no longer recognized such restraint. In them fear—of the lower classes, of communism or simply of change—would turn into an exacerbated fury whose waves would submerge the vacillating framework of the State. Bernanos was then dimly aware of what became a certitude during the Spanish Civil War—that both Maurras and the Church were making grave mistakes: Maurras by alienating definitively the working classes from the ideals of a truly French elite itself linked to the monarchy; the Church by the seemingly realistic calculation that under no circumstances could she lose—that the bourgeoisie, seized by fear before the mounting tide of the revolution, would seek refuge in the arms of the Church. But was this not a faulty reasoning? Bernanos asked. After all, the conservative bourgeois oligarchy, encouraged by the dictatorships—whose extraordinary success neither the Church, nor Bernanos could exactly foresee in the 1920's—might very well prefer other better protected shelters. In that case, the bourgeoisie might exchange the truths of religion for the mystique of fascism. The great unasked question was, would Maurras and the members of the hierarchy then follow the troops they had had the impression of leading?

THE FAILURE OF MAURRAS

When Bernanos gave up his membership at the *Action Française* in 1920, he was by no means detached, intellectually and spiritually, from its ideals. Not only did he keep on writing for it and its various sister publications, but he maintained intimate friendships with many collaborators and sympathizers of Charles Maurras. What, then, was his reaction when the Vatican's judgment struck so unexpectedly against Maurras and his life-work?

We know that Bernanos no longer believed in the restoration of the French elite through the ideas of Maurras. As we shall see, the break between them was going to become deeper until Bernanos discovered, through experience and his inner evolution as a novelist, that Maurras and his "integral nationalism" embodied all the evil that he himself (and Drumont) had ever denounced. Yet, Bernanos had an infinitely generous soul, ready to leap to the defense of a man no matter how justly accused. Furthermore, he well realized that the Vatican's measures against Maurras were dictated, or at least *timed* by political considerations, namely by a desire to give assurances to the Republic concerning the loyalty of ecclesiastic circles. This is why Bernanos, as soon as the Vatican condemnation was made public, hastened to assure Maurras, in two letters published in *La Gazette Française*, that it is not the Church but the enemies of the Church who are bent on his destruction. At the same time he let Maurras know that he was standing by him, with personal friendship and sympathy.

The object of these sentiments, however, was not so much the person of Maurras as the thirty-year struggle, much of which Bernanos still approved. He made this clear in a letter to

Henri Massis, for whom he still felt a great friendship at the time, and who had chosen to remain faithful to Maurras. "I never had for Maurras anything but an admiration without tenderness," Bernanos wrote, "but we must bring him the testimony of our compassion; it was fitting that Maurras should keep silent after the Pope had spoken, but it was doubly necessary for his friends to speak up and to enlighten public opinion."

In December of that year he summed up his reaction in *La Revue fédéraliste:* one must accept unconditionally the decision of the Church, he wrote. Not Maurras alone, but his Catholic friends too ought to do penance: they did not help him with their prayers to cross the threshold of the faith.

In fact, although this is difficult to explain, Bernanos drew closer to the *Action Française* during the years following the condemnation. He continued to write for them and to speak at their meetings—Daudet actually saluted in him the great orator and popular tribune. He obviously enjoyed, in the midst of old friends, the new prestige of the successful novelist. In addition to this, the attitude of those who had obeyed the papal injunction to the letter filled him with disgust; there were those who secretly rejoiced at the opportunity of setting out on their own. Some simply robbed Maurras of his ideas; others retraced their steps and became apologists of democracy. The "desertion" of Jacques Maritain affected Bernanos greatly because he had seen in Maritain the great philosopher who was to "christianize" the Maurrassian doctrine. Now he wrote to Massis: "A new modernist* invasion begins. One hundred years of concessions and equivocations have allowed the spirit of anarchy to penetrate the clergy. . . . One of these days I shall be executed by Bolshevik priests with the *Social Contract* in their pocket and the cross on their breast."[18]

Bernanos' second honeymoon with the *Action Française* may be explained, then, by his independent and chivalrous tempera-

* For Catholics "modernism" had been defined in *The Syllabus of Modern Errors* by Pius IX in 1864.

ment, which forbade him to accept any impositions from however exalted a source, and by his fear, shared at the time by many others, that the condemnation of Maurras would encourage the Left and open the gates to anarchy. But even so this alliance was not to last long.

It was not to last because, for the first time in his life, Bernanos was devoting himself entirely to his novels, and the creation of this world tolerated no other preoccupation. I believe that it was largely through his deepening penetration into the workings of the soul—his knowledge of abbé Donissan and the curé of Ambricourt—that Bernanos acquired his decisive insights into the human and political conflicts which separated his compatriots. Before 1926 he seemed to wage war on forces he could not exactly identify. As a result, his way of writing, despite its eloquence and sincerity, was loose and easily side-tracked. The closer we get to 1936—the writing of the *Diary* and the experiences of the Spanish Civil War—the better aware we become that Bernanos was narrowing his target, that he aimed more precisely, that he had finally found the devil which, in *Sous le Soleil de Satan*, was still somewhat vague. At the same time his youthful arrogance disappeared, and we have before us a man in possession of all his forces which permitted him to be tolerant in his basically intolerant way. The tone became more passionate but it sounded deeper, and anguish crept under the protestations of confidence. A fine web of dialogue elaborated itself slowly through his writings, the dialogue between his temptation, expressed in the question: *à quoi bon*, what is the use? and the answer, uttered at the moment of his death by the curé of Ambricourt: *tout est grâce!*

If we have another glance at his novels, we find essentially two types which preoccupy him and whom I have identified as the *saint* and the *despairing*. Bernanos' interest in and concern for these fictional characters was so intense that it might have been impossible for him not to find human beings among those he knew who embodied, to some extent one or the other type, and, in turn, it is improbable that he did not apply the knowledge he gained by probing the strongly lit souls of his characters to people around him. We know from a passage in one of his works that he fashioned the curé of Ambricourt after the image he had of his own childhood, the abbé Donissan after the curé of Ars, and it is more than likely that Anatole France, the old Zola, André Gide, and as I have said, Maurras himself appear in the guise of other characters.

Why Maurras? Maurras had been young Bernanos' political ideal, the savior who would reunite France with the king, with tradition and with the Church. As he realized that the *Action Française* failed to fulfill any of these promises and that it became not the mouthpiece of an emerging and daring elite, but an abortive growth on the dead tissue of the nation's body, he turned away from the movement and identified himself with an ever smaller part of its aspirations. But he also understood with an artist's intuition that the movement, so inseparable from the person and the personality of Maurras, was indeed the reflection of the latter's soul, and that its entire destiny could be interpreted if one took pains to explore the inner man. Bernanos firmly believed in the intimate harmony and correspondence between the spirit and destiny of a nation (or a class) and certain privileged figures who come to incarnate that spirit and link their existence to that nation's. Thus he found in Luther not only a religious reformer, but also the spirit of Germany which was again manifested in Hitler; and many of his passages testify to his never-ending awe before the fragile figure of Joan of Arc in whom he saw the mystical incarnation of Christian France.

He held Maurras personally responsible for the degeneration of the *Action Française*, and, consequently, he charged him with heavy responsibility for the tragic turn of events later. We shall see in another chapter how Bernanos was to concentrate his attacks on Maurras and the conservatives in general after he had understood what he thought was the bottomless devil-ishness of their spiritual avarice. This understanding came to him during his stay in Majorca while the civil war flared up in Spain. But before that time, in the early 1930's, he seemed to have elaborated for himself an image of Maurras, as yet in-complete, but acquiring increased accuracy as he allowed some of his fictional characters to parade before his inner vision.

I have no doubt that the abbé Cénabre of *L'Imposture* has certain subtle affinities with Charles Maurras. Cénabre is a historian of saints; he has, in other words, a precious charge in his care. He is also a man of considerable authority as a prober of souls, as a man of exceptionally strong will who attracts to himself weaker people whether the wretched journalist com-ing to consult him, or M. de Clergerie, or the *clochard* who attaches himself one night to his steps. But we know also that this man who is seemingly so well armored, who is eminently re-spectable as a scholar and influential as a man of the world, is rotten inside with dryness and is innerly bent by the burden of the stony carapace he forces himself to wear. The mask of his face becomes indistinguishable from his features, and the breath of his spirit, instead of vivifying like the divine breath or the sacerdotal touch, scorches and desiccates the soul which comes in contact with it.

"How is it," Bernanos asked in *Nous autres, Français*, "that at the same time as Maurras destroys the false ideas, he also sterilizes the right ones and empties them of their sap? There is only one answer to this mystery: the Maurrassian spirit is absolutely lacking in charity, I mean to say the charity of Christ."[19] And elsewhere, in *Le Chemin de la Croix-des-Ames*, he exclaims that "the life of Maurras has been one enormous enterprise of corrupting people's consciences." "The truth is," he continues, "that Maurras does not believe in Reason any more than he believes in Monarchy or in the Church. And it would be rash even to say that he believes in himself alone, for he does not believe in himself either, or if he does, it is to hate himself the more. His lucid, icy haughtiness has become, with old age, an instrument of self-torture."[20]

Thus it is easy for Bernanos to establish a passage between his fictional characters and political reality, and it is easy for us to follow him in this enterprise of which, for all we know, he may not even have been fully conscious. The results, however, were there for everybody to see. Starting with 1931, the year of the publication of *La Grande Peur des Bien-Pensants*, Bernanos began his collaboration on François Coty's *Le Figaro*. Coty is still a somewhat mysterious figure in the political-journalistic annals of the Third Republic's most tormented years. The wealthy industrialist of the famous perfume brand considered himself a potential reformer of political life, a healer of the cleavage which was rending the nationalist movement. Anxious to find a strong substitute for the declining power of the *Action Française*, he began by encouraging Colonel de la Rocque and subsidizing his *Croix de Feu* movement, various right-wing causes and publications. Finally, he was even considering the possibility of making his own publications a center of national revival, a kind of intellectual clearing ground from which a purer wind was to blow onto the dreary flatland of democratic parliamentarism. Bernanos, disappointed in Maurras and universally recognized now as a great Catholic novelist, was approached and offered a leading role in the recruitment of men who would wish to form the elite of writers and publicists attached to the cause.

It was only natural that *l'Action Française* should turn its batteries against Coty and take Bernanos to task for cooperating with him, that is, in the usual language of the paper, for *betraying* the forces of integral nationalism. For reasons other than these attacks, Bernanos decided, early in the following year (1932), to part company with Coty and give up his desk at the *Figaro;* but the whole year was spent, anyway, in exchanges of open letters between him and the editors of *l'Action Française*, letters which Bernanos continued publishing in two of Coty's newspapers, *Le Figaro* and *L'Ami du Peuple*.

Bernanos' brief presence at the side of Coty is significant for two reasons: in the exchange of open letters is written the history of the break between him and the Maurrassian movement—its motives and its inevitable violence; and in the relationship which brought the writer and the publisher together, we may study Bernanos' political evolution.

L'Action Française used their habitual method of attack by implying that Bernanos, always known for his lack of funds, had sold himself. As far as the industrialist was concerned, it seems that the anathema had been pronounced on him, first, for being an independent force, not linked to Maurras, and second, for wanting to bring about a *union nationale* of the Right *and* of "men of good will" on the Left within the framework of the Republican state.

That the initiative of Coty was judged important became clear from the fact that Maurras himself took up the pen against Bernanos, whom he called, in an article entitled *"Un Adieu,"* renegade. He then proceeded to enumerate Bernanos' links to various *Action Française*-sponsored organizations, his misbehavior (alleged attacks against the Orleans-branch of the dynasty) and his forced resignation. Much was brought up during this anti-Bernanos compaign obviously designed to destroy the writer's reputation, to isolate him, and thereby to cancel the value of his collaboration to Coty. Statements of Bernanos were quoted, for example, indicating that he considered Coty a "good catch," a money bag from which even *l'Action Française* might have a share, particularly since Maurras, as quoted by Bernanos, had admitted that he too "would accept money from the devil himself for his newspaper."

On his part, Bernanos replied by asserting the sincerity and

voluntary nature of his break with Maurras and by maintaining
that a "French royalist may write in *Le Figaro* without having
to compromise his loyalty." The tone of the letters from the
other side, however, was so violent and so personal, that Bernanos could not keep this increasingly ugly correspondence on
a higher, theoretical level. Since his convictions were questioned, he counter-attacked by examining Maurras' credentials
as a self-appointed defender of monarchy and religion. At the
age of fifteen, he wrote, Maurras was already dreaming of a
universal theocracy: "In this ferocious, almost insane insistence
on *order* in a young child, who can miss detecting the fatal sign,
the bad augury of Christian sentiments already rotting in the
heart of his formal Catholicism?" Maurras is not a Christian
in the full and generous sense of the word, but a Dominican
monk of the thirteenth century who pronounces anathemas and
excommunicates his personal enemies. His loyalty goes only
so far as the recognition of his leadership by others: in spite
of his professed royalism, he forced, by his *non possumus* of
1908, the Pretender to yield to his own doctrine and strategy;
and he brandished another *non-possumus* in 1926, this time in
the Pope's face. "There is only one thing Maurras expects of
history;" he wrote to Coty in November 1932, "that it should
confirm his predictions."

Personal and vicious as the tone of the debate was, behind it
we may now see the dispassionate, lucid evaluation of the
Action Française movement by Bernanos. Bernanos asked himself, in the first place, whether behind the entire anti-Coty-
Bernanos campaign there was not a subtle attempt to push Coty
towards the Left and to enroll in the camp of the *Action
Française* the nationalist readers who would then abandon *Le
Figaro*. He estimated that the years of the movement were
numbered, but he also acknowledged that Maurras still had
some trump cards: a camp of fanatic followers, an enormous
literary and intellectual prestige and the very method of at-

tack of which he himself was feeling the impact at the time.* All in all, he advised Coty not to underestimate his adversaries: "*L'Action Française* may no longer be able to do much good, but it remains powerful when it comes to doing evil." Then he suggested means of destroying the movement by alienating from it the Pretender and the public. He realized that it was necessary to suggest *tactical* moves instead of *doctrinal* ones, since he himself had experienced the magnetism of the Maurrassian doctrines. He knew, therefore, that it would be a mistake to launch a frontal attack against doctrines which were "a skillful synthesis of the last hundred years' national political experience" with deep roots in various classes of society.

Bernanos did not deny that he admired this synthesis and that he had gone along with its conclusions as long as it had not assumed the status of dogma in the Maurrassian Church. In other words, he did not mean to repudiate the entire line of the *Action Française* as it had been elaborated between 1905 and 1914. Neither did he wish to repudiate all of his own youthful commitments. What he did want to do was in harmony with his own spiritual-political evolution since 1919: cleanse the Maurrassian movement of its post-war impurities, and since that could not be done in the framework of the *Action Française*, create at *Le Figaro* the necessary conditions for such a restoration. "We must make of Figaro the sole intellectual center of Paris," he wrote Coty; "the youth, the intellectuals, the public and ultimately the Pretender himself—will rally to us."

Although nothing came of the project, there is nothing surprising in this optimism or in the attempt to create a new movement by digging down to the original roots of nationalism. It was not the only one of its kind in the early 1930's. There were organized movements which tried to take the succession of the *Action Française* by profiting from its doctrine, its partisans

* For the sake of comparison, *l'Action Française* had, at the time, approximately thirty-thousand readers, *Le Figaro*, 500 thousand.

and its prestige and bringing some of its ideas up to date—and the daily or weekly publications like *Je suis partout, Gringoire, Candide* (violently anti-British, pro-Mussolini, anti-Semitic). And there were many attempts, preceded by innumerable and long debates, at recreating the *Bloc national*, right-wing unity, understanding among patriots and so on. Even the writer Jules Romains, trusting his prestige and connections in France, Italy and Germany, tried his hand at assembling some young and brilliant intellectuals into a movement to check France's decadence and leftward switch.

"RATHER HITLER THAN BLUM"

These were the months and years of crystallization for both Left and Right, and therefore all attempts like that of Coty and Bernanos to find a solution somewhere at the middle were naturally thwarted. The increasingly felt presence of Soviet Russia sent shudders through the social and economic consciousness of the French middle classes, while the rise of Nazism in Germany alarmed their nationalist sensibilities. The problem could almost be formulated by asking which of the two, the fear of Russia or the fear of Germany, was to determine the final decision. The slogan: "Rather Hitler than Blum," was soon to show the choice.

The depression spreading from the United States was another decisive factor. Beyond the actual misery and economic collapse that it caused, more thoughful elements in intellectual circles were forced to see in the depression a confirmation of Marxist predictions concerning the evermore serious crises rocking western capitalism. At the same time, Soviet Russia initiated its first Five-Year Plan, demonstrating thereby that the first ten years of experimentation with various economic measures had not weakened the communist leaders' will to build socialism in a rational way. Even those who questioned the inhuman means used by these leaders had to admit that the increasing number of unemployed, their present distress and bleak future were not of a nature to prove the superiority of the capitalistic system over communism.

These agitating problems called forth two responses on the part of nationalist-rightist bourgeoisie in France: the more general response came out of the immediate, almost instinctive fear of the working classes and the reforms advocated by the leftist parties—the communists, socialists and left-wing Radicals. The second, more intellectual and articulate response, was dictated by the need to counteract the influence of Marxism among the working classes and intellectuals. It aimed at creating a movement—an organization and a consciousness— which would be at once social-minded, nationalistic in inspiration and protective of the values of western civilization and Christendom.

These two "responses" cannot be clearly separated. In retrospect we can see that the first, middle-class anxiety, found its *historic* culmination in the second, a form of fascist ideology. But we can best follow the process by separating the two responses according to the leading personalities who embodied them.

We shall speak of the fascist ideology in France—and Bernanos' reaction to it—in the next chapter; let us now look, briefly and through Bernanos' analysis, at the more elusive bourgeois attitude in the early 1930's.

When I say "analysis," I realize that this term has an unusual meaning when applied to Bernanos' writings. Bernanos was not a detached novelist, but one who lived with his characters. He therefore was never able, or willing, to deal with human beings *or groups* as with impersonal blocks and forces. Bernanos talks to, about or against the bourgeoisie as if it were a person endowed with an individual conscience, a sense of responsibility and feelings of guilt, honor and ambition. By "personalizing" the nation and its various interest and pressure groups, Bernanos builds up a drama in which flesh and blood

actors confront each other, and which is more true to life than
a dispassionate study would be.

Outside of this power of animation, Bernanos analyzed the
ideological evolution of the French middle classes much as a
social philosopher would. This means that he understood the
deep bourgeois commitment to progress through science and
production, a progress which in their eyes only sentimental or
power-crazy worker-agitators would dare disturb. He understood, in other words, the mentality reflected in Jules Ferry's
remark: "The working class better understand that its only
hope is in resignation." As a reward for accepting this paternalistic attitude, the working class was assured that its most talented
members would find their way to economic and even social
emancipation, equivalent, of course, to abandoning their class of
origin in an unorganized, leaderless condition. This is how M.
Albert Guérard describes the place of the working masses in
what he calls the "Republic of Jules Ferry": "The masses were
to be taught the three R's; but secondary education, the gate-
way to all the professions, was made neither compulsory nor
free. It remained the preserve of the middle class, protected
both by custom and by a financial barrier. A worker's son could
hope to become a better mechanic, artisan or foreman, a clerk,
a small shopkeeper, an elementary teacher; but only in exceptional cases could he aspire to be a civil engineer, a manager,
a professor, a doctor, a judge, a diplomat, or an army officer.
The few who conquered all obstacles were expected to forget
their proletarian origin and aggregate themselves with the
bourgeoisie. Full equality of opportunity was not even at-
tempted until after World War I; then it was bitterly combated
as demagogic and extravagant."[21]

The bourgeois organization of society was suddenly called
into question by socialism—that is, not merely the *right* of the
bourgeoisie to organize the world, but even its efficiency and
historical justification. The leaders of the middle class, wrote
Bernanos, were staggered by the denunciations of Marx who

condemned them "precisely in the name of Science and History." However, although this may seem a paradox, they were saved once more by the Dreyfus case and by the Ralliement: "In fact, they were saved twice: first, by securing again the rule of radical bourgeoisie over the working class, in the name of the Defense of the Republic [against the enemies of Dreyfus]; second, by permitting a handful of intellectuals to deviate the Christian Socialist movement towards nationalism."[22]

But the most respectable support came from the Church which, "in its turn, condemned the materialism of Marx; the materialism of bourgeois economic liberalism suddenly appeared in a more favorable light. It was natural for the bourgeoisie to rally then to the Church. . . . The priests . . . provided them with a better conscience. What had the bourgeois been guilty of, anyway? Only of some abuses of the Right of Property. But the socialist adversaries were attacking not the abuses but the very principle of ownership! In the defense of this sacred right, the bourgeoisie, materialist as it was, found itself on the side of the world's greatest spiritual power."[23] "Throughout the nineteenth century," Bernanos was to write in a Brazilian review, in 1943, "members of the clergy had uselessly compromised with liberal society and liberal economy, hoping to win over the Voltairean middle class which grew, with every passing day, richer and more powerful. The Encyclical *Rerum Novarum* came too late, much too late, while the fortunes of Marxism were getting high. The Church thus seemed to listen to the just claims [of working classes] at the very moment when the latter was becoming strong enough to impose respect on their employers without anybody's help."[24]

When, after World War I, Communism appeared on the stage, the actors of the drama were strengthened in their roles. "Until 1918 the bourgeoisie could still entertain some doubts as to the authenticity of its apostolic mission; the emergence of Communism confirmed it definitively as the veritable Eldest Daughter of the Church." And the Church tacitly approved this display of bad faith: "The Jesuits seemed to say: 'once we enroll these bourgeois in one of our organizations, we will have time to enlighten them!' "[25]

Thus, in Bernanos' estimation, the middle classes were only interested in their economic privileges and in vague, Pharisaic "good conscience" which, in a Catholic country, made of them the doubtful allies of the Church. But Bernanos could not believe in bourgeois *conviction* separate from bourgeois *interests;* his views are almost Marxist in their interpretation of bourgeois attitudes, slogans and alliances, because, in his eyes, those who sacrifice to Mammon are so corrupt as to become blind to values, even to their own ideological values. Alliance with religion had to be, necessarily, brief and inconclusive. In *Les Enfants humiliés* he warned the clergy not to offer a shelter for the protection of bourgeois interests because the bourgeoisie will not stop there but will go on towards the more promising camp of the dictators.

In *Lettre aux Anglais*,[26] a few years later, he registered the shift. This is how he retraced, with a few vivid brushstrokes, the change from a vaguely religious pose to a more frank, reactionary attitude: "All throughout the nineteenth century the bourgeois refused to admit that their discord with the people made them bitter. Yet, the term 'reactionary' was to them a term of shame because it seemed to dishonor them in the eyes of the intellectuals. And even when the intellectuals began to rehabilitate both the term and the thing, this attempt utterly confused them. In Maurrassism they saw, at first, a café paradox, a farce from the Provence. Not that they disliked the ideas of this little man, infirm, cunning and perverse, one of the most sinister of our history; but they only dared approach these ideas in secret, the way one goes to a house of prostitution."

Then came, as a blow to the bourgeois republic even while the war was going on, the collapse of Russia and with it the cancellation, by the Communist government, of French investments and loans contracted by the Tsarist regime since the

1890's: "The collapse of the Russian loan," Bernanos noted, "coincided with the outbreak of Communist propaganda. This double fact had the result of definitively separating the petty bourgeoisie from the working class, and of pushing the former towards the high middle class."

This is how the support of Maurrassism grew with every new shock experienced by the middle classes, low or high. And this is how Maurras, while imagining that he was in control, became, in reality, the instrument of forces which flattered his intellectual pride and will for power. "The French leading circles," wrote Bernanos, ". . . did not give a damn about the theses of integral nationalism which, for them, had never been more than a *divertissement* for intellectuals. From the neo-patriotism of Maurras all they wanted to retain was the principle which inspired it: *par tous les moyens;* this principle had long been their motto in business, but they never dared proclaim it in public. Now M. Maurras freed them of this sense of shame."

Bernanos' break with the *Action Française* merely confirmed what was to be expected from such a disparate relationship. The movement wore, throughout its existence, the stamp of Maurras' personality and ideas, and I hope it is clear to the reader by now that the presence of Bernanos in its ranks was essentially incongruous. With the usual idealism of generous men, Bernanos had attributed the *values* he believed in and the *qualities* he possessed to the *Action Française* (in a way, like those left-wing idealists who lent the Communist Party their own good intentions until some eye-opening experience); but his attachment was never really to the conceptual universe of Maurras, much less to the practical policies that Maurras advocated and justified.

Personally, as we have seen from his letter to Massis, he did not like Maurras, although he felt a certain affinity with Léon Daudet who was a sensitive man and an artist like himself. Also, he had many friends who were in the movement or close to it, and Bernanos was a man who could identify himself passionately with a minority, especially with men whose background and inbred reflexes were like his own.

In 1938–39 two events occurred which suddenly turned the tide which had been, since 1926, unfavorable to Maurras. First, he posed his candidacy and was admitted to the French Academy; then, in the following year, under the new pope's rule, the condemnation against the *Action Française* was rescinded. Nobody doubted that Maurras' literary merits were amply sufficient for receiving such an honor, but everybody understood that his membership in the sanctuary of the Quai Conti was a great victory for the Right, indeed a nationally significant event. Reconciliation with the Vatican confirmed this impression, and it seemed, in addition, to reward Maurras' tenacity.

But if Bernanos, in 1926, had brought his loyal support to the Maurras whom everybody wanted to abandon, he now acted again in complete independence and with absolute contempt for the opportunists; "as soon as the political circumstances made a reconciliation between the *Action Française* and the Church desirable," writes Urs von Balthasar of this period, "Bernanos tore himself away from the movement with a greater violence than before, as if he had meant to protect in himself what was best in the movement. And it is truly this better part that won out in this ex-*camelot du roi* . . . He was to conserve, to the end, the spirit that he himself had introduced in the *Action Française*, that he thought to have discovered there and that he removed now intact: the spirit of French and Catholic form."[27]

NOTES

1. *Les Enfants humiliés*, p. 71.
2. *La France contre les Robots*, pp. 95–7.
3. *Ibid.*, pp. 95, 98.
4. *Nous autres, Français*, p. 97.
5. *Les Grands Cimetières sous la lune*, p. II.

6. Article by Léon Daudet, April 1926. Quoted in *Bulletin*, Nos. 17–20, Christmas 1953.

7. Yves Simon, *The Road to Vichy* (London: Sheed and Ward, 1942), pp. 42–3. See also Bernanos' remarks in *Les Grands Cimetières sous la lune:* in the judgment of the Right "the dictators want the salvation of France, the League of Nations wants her destruction." But why this assumption, Bernanos then asks, about the League of Nations, which we have built and which we still dominate? Why does the Right denounce the treaties and the value of signatures? Why does it rejoice over Mussolini's campaign in Abyssinia?

8. Quoted by Henri Massis, *Evocations* (Plon, 1931), p. 46.

9. *La Droite en France*, p. 202.

10. *Le Chemin de la Croix-des-Ames*, I, p. 86.

11. *Les Grands Cimetières sous la lune*, pp. 63–68.

12. Gaetan Picon, *Georges Bernanos* (Ed. Robert Marin, 1948), p. 172.

13. *Les Grands Cimetières sous la lune*, pp. 49–51.

14. Léon Roudiez, *Maurras jusqu'à l'Action Française* (André Bonne, 1957), p. 280.

15. This sentence is contained in a short autobiographical notice entrusted to a compatriot in Brazil. It was published a few weeks after Bernanos' death under the title of "Autobiographie," in *La Nef*, August 1948.

16. Simone Weil, *L'Enracinement* (Gallimard, 1949), pp. 86–7.

17. P. 34.

18. Henri Massis, *Maurras et son temps* (La Palatine, 1951), p. 174.

19. P. 80.

20. Vol. III, pp. 68–70.

21. Albert Guérard, *France: a Modern History* (Ann Arbor: University of Michigan Press, 1959), p. 341.

22. *Scandale de la vérité*.

23. *Lettre aux Anglais*, pp. 101–103.

24. *Bulletin*, No. 10, June 1952. Note the identity of views of Bernanos and Jaurès in their evaluation of *Rerum Novarum*.

25. *Lettre aux Anglais*, pp. 101–103.

26. See pp. 93–4, 107, 111.

27. *Le Chrétien Bernanos*, pp. 55–6.

4 "The Silent Tomorrow"

AT the end of the last chapter I mentioned the "fascist temptation" as a "second response" to the challenge that nationalist French youth faced in the 1930's. The temptation was not the problem of France alone: before France was to be half-engulfed by it, Italy, Germany and Spain had adopted fascism —or some form of it—as a system; a number of smaller countries, in Central and Eastern Europe, followed their lead.

We may even say that France fared best in that it never fully succumbed to the grossest forms of fascism. Throughout this period, it remained in France an intellectual exercise or *ideology*, not a *creed* as in Germany, nor a *regime* as in Italy. The probable reason for this was, in M. René Rémond's words, that France had, despite the upheavals rocking the surface, a basically stable society: "For a handful of fascists, there was a minority of reactionaries and an immense majority of conservatives."[1]

This was not the case either in Germany or in Spain, the two countries whose example was so important for France during the fateful decade. Italian fascism, in spite of the great admiration which the French Right had for Mussolini, his corporatist regime and his Abyssinian campaign, made no deep impression on the rightist intellectuals; first because there was very little in common between the two countries' intellectual and literary tradition—despite the Latin bond uniting the two sister nations—and, second, because they felt that fascism had never impregnated the youth of Italy, its writers and intellectuals in the manner in which at least part of the German and Spanish elite were affected by their respective nationalist movements, National Socialism and Falangism.

There were substantial differences in the 1930's between the outlook and mentality of French, German, Italian and Spanish middle classes, yet the over-all feeling of alarm before the mounting tide of socialism and communism was almost identical. The behavior of these classes can, therefore, be understood and their course charted by realizing that their state of mind was dominated by *fear* which, in Bernanos' interpretation, was increasingly turning into *fury (colère)*. *Les Grands Cimetières sous la lune*, his second great denunciation of French bourgeoisie (1937), with *La Grande Peur* (1931) traces the history of this great fear from 1848 to the 1930's and its progression to frenzy. "Fear, real fear, is a furious delirium," he wrote in *Les Grands Cimetières*, describing the mental anguish of the Spanish middle class and finding, on the Iberian peninsula, obvious parallels with the same class in his own country.

It cannot be emphasized often enough that fascism was not so much a reaction against communism as against democracy. It is a too-little mentioned fact that many leaders of the fascist and National-Socialist parties were men who had previously been socialists and, in a number of cases, communists. This neglect may be due to a conscious effort on the part of the socialist as well as bourgeois historians to conceal the preoccupation of these, later criminally involved, individuals with any kind of genuine working-class interest. The truth is, nevertheless, that Mussolini in Italy, Marcel Déat, Adrian Marquet, Laval and Doriot in France and Henri de Man in Belgium began their political careers as militants in the ranks of socialism, and renounced their loyalty only after failing to reform the Party from within on a line different from orthodox Marxism. It is no exaggeration to say that, on many points and for some time during the early 1920's, socialism and the fascist splinter groups had quite a lot in common, and that the bases of Marxist criticism of capitalism and democracy offered a platform on which extreme Right and extreme Left were able to stand together. Georges Sorel himself, the founder of Syndicalism, observed with sympathy and satisfaction the beginnings of both Leninist Russia and the Italy of Mussolini. These new, anti-capitalistic and anti-parliamentary regimes had been born from the same earth-shaking and mass-moving myth, proletarian violence. And violence, according to Sorel, was not to exhaust itself in a mere revolt of the workers; he believed, as did Marx, that the proletarian revolution would destroy both economic liberalism and bourgeois democracy. It would produce a new *juridical* frame for the State and culminate in the establishment of a *work-morality*, indeed a religion.

It is significant to read, in this respect, the address of the Fascist Pavolini at the Foreign Policy Congress in Milan in June, 1938. Summing up the work of the convention, Pavolini declared: "Nothing irritates us so much as to be taken for pillars of order. Nothing so exasperates us as the people who come to us through fear of Communism." The speaker went on by quoting from the review *Gerarchia,* founded by Mussolini: "Those good people [who are fearful of all social change] will have to realize, and we shall soon make them realize, that the weight of the social problem is now on our shoulders and that they would be wiser to fear us than to fear communism."[2]

Similar examples of kinship between socialism (or communism) and various forms of fascism, as well as their common hatred of democracy and the bourgeois state, can be found in Germany. There too, a parallel movement can be detected: the middle classes, ruined by war, revolution and inflation, flocked to Hitler out of fear of Bolshevization. But the nationalist elite (which was not necessarily the same as the Nazi elite) seemed to prefer communism to the weak, degenerate Weimar Republic, even if they too had to end up in Hitler's camp. "Unless it were possible to re-create a form of State," wrote Ernst von Salomon, "Bolshevism must be the natural heir to the obvious and shameless dissolution of all organic strength by the ideological senselessness of the bourgeois-liberal and Social-Democrat wizards."[3]

Drieu la Rochelle in France was to echo, some twelve years later, this almost spiteful expectation of the inevitable Russian avalanche. As a disillusioned collaborator of the Germans, he wrote in 1943: "The only power capable of replacing Germany in Europe is Russia . . . So then, in the end, it is the Russian who will cry, on a tone astonishingly perverse, seductive and crushing: 'It is we, Europe! Europe to the Europeans! Anglo-Saxons, get out!'. . . . I believe that if the Russians arrived in France, the mere breath of their vitality would suffice to blow us Frenchmen away."[4]

The same hope of strengthening the State by closing the gap that the bourgeoisie had opened in the body of society was sounded by the best elements of the Spanish *Falange* movement. We shall see later how Bernanos, a witness of the Spanish Civil War in Majorca, distinguished between the ardent young idealists who joined the Falange and the reactionary bourgeoisie behind Franco who forced them into the reactionary ranks of the Army. The young Mateo Santos, in Gironella's great novel, *The Cypresses Believe in God,* joins the Falange, prompted by a deep-felt loyalty to José Antonio, its founder, and by the ideals which were identical to those expressed by Ernst von Salomon, namely of re-creating the State, reintegrating the workers into the body of the nation, and fighting with them for social justice. The Falange's aim was, he explains to friends, to convince the workers that they were not proletarians but men, *persons*. Second, to persuade them that the economic aspect is not the only one, and that once the material needs were taken care of thousands of spiritual roads opened to them. Third, to inspire them with love of family and work; and fourth, to give them a great collective illusion which would keep them from starting a revolution every other day for paltry reasons. "Above all," Mateo ended his talk, "the Falange believed in sacrifice, it was a mystique, a total concept of life."[5]

THE DESPAIRING ACTIVISTS

The French candidates to fascism had a head-start over their German, Italian and Spanish contemporaries. In Maurras, although he never was a fascist, they had found the most brilliant exponent of nationalism and rightist doctrine and a prestigious blend of all the ideas which had secretly or openly appealed to their middle-class education and cultural heritage, their concept of an elite, and their indignation over the inequities and materialism of the modern world. In Maurras' retinue there were some brilliant young writers: Céline, Bardèche, Brasillach, Thierry Maulnier and Drieu La Rochelle—all of them frustrated over their political impotence, while in Germany, Italy and Spain men of their generation were involved in epic battles for changing the world. In their literary works this frustration often assumed the form of an obsession, of cynical exasperation and, not rarely, of vague, prophetic vision. The feeling of political impotence expressed itself in a fervor to destroy the existing frame of society and its most repulsive symptom, bourgeois morality. When they hailed Mussolini, Hitler and Franco as saviors of a decadent Europe, this was, among other things, their way of translating a nostalgic longing for participation in shaping their nations' destinies. "I am a fascist," exclaimed Drieu La Rochelle, "because I have measured the progress of decadence in Europe."

These were the men who fought on the other side of the barricade in February 1934, hailed Hitler against Blum, flocked to Franco's army instead of the International Brigade and could hardly conceal their joy at the French surrender in June 1940 in which they saw the just punishment of a servile and decadent regime. The Stalin-Hitler pact itself, which created a wave of moral collapse among fellow-travelers and split the

French Communist Party, provoked in their camp elation and confident expectation. What honest communists like Paul Nizan could not accept from Stalin, Hitler's French admirers received as a new guarantee of the Führer's brilliant Machiavellism.

Hitler and his Germans represented the "new Barbarians" that a Drieu was eager to welcome, for they were supposed to bring with them a clean and healthy vigor, shaking life into "modern man whose highest ambition and achievement was the sexual act." More than that, fascism was to restore the rule of the elite over the "dispirited masses that have remained without spiritual guidance and moral authority." This is, of course, an echo of Sorel's teaching, rejecting the illusion of progress and expecting a new (proletarian) elite to impose new molds on society.

But to what extent did Drieu and his companions believe in the possibility of such an elite? In other words, what did they expect of a revolution, *their* revolution? The same question might have been asked of those who were fighting on the other side of the barricade. The difference between the two sides was not so great; it became emphasized in the strong light cast upon it by subsequent events. These young men, the elite of France, held basically the same values (or, one should perhaps say, *anti-values*); often some secondary factors and earlier experiences decided whether loyalty to these values led one man into one camp rather than into another. Speaking in general, Henri Massis, who was well-placed to watch the entire parade of this generation, had this to say about them: "These young men get involved in combats where they go to test their courage and satisfy their taste for masculine comradeship. They seek out these battles only to avenge themselves on life's absurdity, to escape the abyss by throwing themselves into it. This is what makes all these young men seem alike: whether they are fascists or anti-fascists: they are all despairing activists!"[6] Massis then calls attention to a short character-description of values, manifest in French fascism, from the pen of Etienne Borne, an anti-fascist Catholic philosopher. It is hard to detect anything in this description that would not apply to the feelings and convictions of other young men on the Left: the values that M. Borne recognizes in fascism are "the contempt for the trivial and the routine, the search for grandeur, the refusal of a mendacious idealism which hides a comfortable and prosperous egoism under universal morality. An effort to elaborate an idea of order by tearing it away from bourgeois compromises; finally, the certainty that there are reasons to live which are worth more than life itself."[7]

Thus, among intellectuals at least, fascism, like communism, was an attempt to give shape—and an organizational form—to their revolt against the middle class, bourgeois values, the profit mentality and phony idealism. The term "democracy" was the most despised target because it represented what was in the eyes of these young men the biggest fraud of all, the pretense to include "the people," the semblance of social justice. "Democracy," wrote Alfred Fabre-Luce, "has become nothing but a propaganda slogan . . . It is the word thrown to citizens who are more and more passive, so as to make them believe that they are masters of their destiny. What is developing underneath is a soulless international bureaucracy."[8] Of one thing everybody was sure: democracy and bourgeois society were not worth defending, were not worth fighting for. Shortly before the war, Bernanos wrote in the posthumously published *Les Enfants humiliés:* "From the extreme Right to the extreme Left, with the exception of a few happy mediocrities, decorated impostors, bigots and lackeys, and bureaucratic minds, the least one can say is that modern society finds very few to justify and defend it."[9]

Let us remember, at this point, the mood of Bernanos' generation in the post-war months as described at the beginning of the previous chapter. Historically both fascism and National-Socialism grew directly out of post-war disillusionment, nourished by national humiliation and the feeling of misused energy and enthusiasm. While Mussolini's shock-troops were fighting communist infiltration in the northern, industrial districts, various half-demobilized troops and squads in Germany (especially from the Baltic areas) fought the communist spartakists and the socialists of Kurt Eisner in Bavaria.

The situation in France was, of course, different, since France was on the winning side; yet, there remained equivocation about victory and doubt about the organization of internal peace. Bernanos and his more lucid contemporaries felt that the conflict had not been solved; it was merely postponed. If someone had taken the trouble of organizing them, of calling them back to discipline, Bernanos wrote later, "they would have again become an army with its leaders, its argot and inflexible comradeship, as capable of bad as of good. They would have given this army the name of a party, and Europe would have counted one more form of fascism. There was something we did not understand at the time: wars in the past were wars between soldiers; but modern war, total war, is an activity of the totalitarian State, and the soldiers are its human material. This war shapes a new species of man, well broken in, resigned not to understand, not to try to understand. . . . Total war is cruel and puritanical, it gives rise . . . to a type of man who is capable of all forms of submission and violence, going with indifference from one to the other. . . . I do not say that with its admirable methods of deforming consciences modern society would not have brought about, even in peace time, such a totalitarian man: but let us admit that the war speeded up considerably his maturation process."[10]

Does all this mean that fascism was, when everything is said and done, a negative attitude, able to nourish itself on the ruins of a bourgeois society that it had contributed to destroy, but incapable of overcoming its self-generated temptation of despair and nihilism?

The truth is that in fascism both aspects, the positive and

the negative, were represented. Undeniably, it was, particularly in France, a search for a new elite, a stable point from which social order could be re-created. Bernanos, who loathed fascism, recognized, nevertheless, the idealist ingredient in it: "If so many good men are today nazis, fascists or communists," he wrote, "this is because they could not resist the voice of temptation: 'give me everything,' the Party whispered into their ears, 'and I shall restore your honor.' Hearing this, they gave everything with a joyous heart, they even gave their souls."[11]

In *The Diary of a Country Priest*, written in 1935, Bernanos introduces, for the space of a brief but poignant episode, Olivier de Sommerange, a young nobleman. The episode disrupts the narrative, and its insertion in the novel cannot be explained by any consideration of composition or structure. This means that Bernanos felt he had something important to say with this episodic character, the symbol of youth as he wished it had been, as a sort of transposed Joan of Arc for whom the age had no use. Olivier, then, is the last of the knights, the Christian soldier defending honor, country and the faith. But, he tells the priest, "the Church had abandoned us when it delivered Joan of Arc, the perfect type of the Christian soldier, to the secular power"; it has, since then, delivered the whole flower of French youth to the lay State. They are no longer knights but functionaries of the State, military personnel: "We defend the land and we repress street riots; but when the riot wins out, we serve the new regime. The army no longer has any meaning, nor have your treaties and concordats with the Caesars. The ancient State had died together with the gods. As for the gods of the modern State, we know who they are: they dine in town every night, and are called bankers."[12]

What remained for an Olivier or a Gilles (the young hero of Drieu La Rochelle's novel in 1931) to do? Drieu echoed Olivier's disillusioned question: "Without gods who are dead, and without masters who are not yet born, we have nothing except youth. In what else may we believe?"[13]

They believed in revolution and man reborn, but, remarks André Rousseaux, as the new society and the new man remained obstinately absent, their hope turned into bitter despair and into hatred of all things that seemed to delay them. Rejecting their fathers' ideals as well as the modern world, Gilles and Olivier were cornered by the events, and, having an increasingly weaker hold on the present and on the future, they escaped into the past or into a heroic, useless death. Convinced that "the only places that move the heart are churches and wars," Olivier joins the Foreign Legion and predicts before the curé that he will soon fall on the field of honor; Gilles, putting his trust in the day when "the dictators will pay homage to the resurrected Christ," goes off to Franco's Spain and into an impossible battle for "Hitler's socialism" and for the "international of nationalisms."

Thus idealism and the search for a "new honor" led to despair or, at least, to renunciation, resignation and retreat from active (political) life. "I have nothing to do in an age when honor is punished," exclaims the Lord of Santiago in Montherlant's drama, "when everything that is great is belittled and mocked, when the stupid and the abject are assured of their triumph."[14]

The restoration of their sense of honor, the sentiments befitting the elite they considered themselves to be, was of primary importance. Repugnant as they found Soviet Russia and the communist experience, they nevertheless admired a system which was built around the core of a strong ideal, which challenged the youthful enthusiasm of a whole nation, and provided a firm organization the world over for progressive elements. The Catholic faith, the respected concept of family, and an education inspired by western values prevented most young nationalists from ever advocating an alliance with communism; but in those men of the same generation who had overcome such scruples or who had some link with socialism in their past, the ideological differences between National Socialism and communism were not essential. What *was* essential for them was that both systems announced the future while bourgeois democracy was lying on its death-bed, and that this future was guaranteed by the ruthless efficiency with which both Russia and Germany proceeded to shape their own and the world's destiny.

THE ''MANAGERIAL STATE''

Mr. James Burnham achieved considerable fame—and a sort of *succès de scandale*—in 1941 with the publication of his *Managerial Revolution* in which he argued that the three world systems then competing against each other—bourgeois capitalism, national socialism and Soviet communism—tended, in reality, towards an identical form of the bureaucratic state managed by ideologically neutral, highly competent men. These "managers" tended, according to Burnham's analysis, to combine the dying private entrepreneurial system with state-owned corporations, so that in the end they would become semi-public bureaucrats, influencing the affairs of society from its nerve-centers and without actually or formally owning the means of production.

Men like Doriot, Pucheu, Marion, Benoist-Méchin, Philipe Henriot and even Drieu La Rochelle were obviously influenced by theories similar to those of Burnham. They saw themselves as the leaders of the coming managerial state in the new Europe freed of English mercantilism, but freed also of Hitler's misty ideology. It would be organized on the basis of the inevitable compromise (as they saw it) between Bolshevism and the national idea. For a time, under the Vichy regime, the above-mentioned men were reportedly forming a *synarchy* and preparing for the great post-war transformation and the roles they expected to play in the new order. But as early as the 1930's, many had made the switch, partly from conviction, partly to be on the bandwagon. Particularly after the Right's spectacular failure in the events of February 6, 1934, those who felt in themselves the stuff of leadership—and who wanted to save France from the Popular Front—broke with the moderate forms of conservative politics and with liberal Catholicism and opted openly for fascism. This was true of communist leader Jacques Doriot; the politicians Léon Bérard, Philipe Henriot, André Tardieu and the men who were later referred to in Vichy as *les jeunes cyclistes* on account of their ruthless determination to pedal their way to undisputed power. In 1935, after trying to govern France three times as prime minister, André Tardieu, one of the most prominent right-wing politicians, expressed the view that the political situation could not be improved through legal means; the parliamentary regime was in conflict with the country, and the constitutional organs, instead of correcting the defects of the regime, suffered its abuses.[15] Tardieu was soon to resign from Parliament where, in his judgment, he could achieve nothing useful.

Jacques Doriot chose an even more radical way and his example may be taken as typical. A skilled metal worker, Doriot rose rapidly in the ranks of the communist youth organization, became deputy and secretary general of the Party and a friend of Trotsky. For not following, at the right time, Stalin's tortuous policy between socialists and fascists, he was driven from the Party (1934). He then founded the *Parti Populaire Français* which became the rallying point for the well-to-do and the intellectually inclined among the extremist sympathizers.* The logic of events was to push Doriot closer and closer to National Socialism, and during, the occupation, to collaboration. His life ended on a highway in Germany when his car was machine-gunned by an allied airplane in the last months of the war.

* Bernanos mentions that de Jouvenel and Drieu tried to enroll him also in Doriot's party when he was in Majorca.

The difference in tone and degree of maturity between *La Grande Peur des Bien-Pensants* and *Les Grands Cimetières sous la lune* is considerable because in the first—through a lightly sketched biography of Drumont—Bernanos described a class, the nineteenth-century bourgeoisie, of which he had no direct knowledge. His denunciations, in spite of the many concrete instances he quoted, sound somewhat vacuous, and his indignation, although sincere and vehement, has an occasional artificial undertone. When he speaks of the "treason" against Drumont, in the last part of the book, the reader feels that this is a standard cliché, a method of writing rather than demonstrable history.

Les Grands Cimetières sous la lune, on the other hand, takes up the theme of the previous book, but this time Bernanos spoke of his own experiences, observations and reactions. To put it in another way, he himself is the Drumont of his work; he saw the events he described with his own eyes, not those of someone else. The stage setting may be the same: like *La Grande Peur,* the new book reads like a drama. Not only are the individual actors sharply characterized, but the collective protagonists are outlined as if they had one personality and consciousness and, above all, one responsibility before the nation. However, these characters and the distribution of their roles, their guilt or innocence, are not the same as in the book written six years before: it is not the Jews but the conservatives, not the socialists but the Spanish clergy, not Blum but Franco who are the targets of his attack.

Les Grands Cimetières sous la lune was written after Bernanos' eye-opening Majorcan experiences. The reason he was so struck by what he saw was that he understood the similarity between the French and the Spanish situations, and feared that the same forces were going to bring about the same clash and civil war in France that he witnessed in Spain. His system of reference, throughout the book, remained France and French society, and, in this sense, it is almost a didactic and prophetic work, one of Bernanos' finest and most vehement, wrought with the profound anguish of the patriot.

For Bernanos, the years between his final break with the *Action Française* and the move to Majorca to 1935 were quite restless. In 1933 there occurred the motorcycle accident which left his legs in an almost paralytic state. Financially he was not very well off; the important position he had counted upon to occupy at *Le Figaro* did not materialize, and his family could not be supported on his writing alone. He still found writing painful to pursue even though he could not live without it. For these reasons and also because of his increasing bitterness over the state of France, Bernanos decided to move to the Balearic Islands, to Palma de Majorca, where the cost of living was low, where he would be surrounded by the Spanish whom he loved and where he could devote himself to the great novel he now intended to write and which became *The Diary of a Country Priest*.

Much in Bernanos' life had prepared him to take the fascist detour, even after Maurras' hold on him weakened. This is what happened to many of his closest friends and to other members of his generation who had had the same upbringing, literary career, sense of honor and religious faith. Even after the Vatican condemnation of the *Action Française*, Catholics were apt to make a compromise between conscience and political convictions, and many of them were sympathetic to fascism. What is more, there was a danger that, on account of their authoritative tone, pro-fascist journalists and writers were taken for spokesmen of official Catholicism. This danger prompted Bernanos, as he wrote later, to raise the voice of a solitary witness to be heard in Rome and in the world at large, the testimony of a Catholic who did not succumb to the fascist temptation: "there is always a Catholic fascism, a powerful Catholic fascist public opinion. When we mention it, we are immediately accused of hurting the Church. What has hurt the Church is that fascists have spoken in it too long and on the tone of authority. In our turn, we are quite resolved to raise our voice, not to outshout them, but to be heard everywhere, even by Rome."[16]

The fascist temptation was the black fruit of the despair which had seized his generation after 1918 and of which *Les Enfants humiliés* is a moving testimony. The revolution, the transformation which was expected in vain, and the victory which miscarried were at the root of a Drieu's denunciations, of Céline's great satanic novel, *Voyage au bout de la nuit*, and even of Bernanos' own *Under the Sun of Satan*. But while Drieu, Céline and the others were finally engulfed by the logic of their stand, Bernanos was saved by his charity. "Drieu lacked the stuff of hope which is of a spiritual nature," wrote André Rousseaux a few years ago in *Le Figaro Littéraire*. "Bernanos could speak of 'France's surrender' and warn us in terrible terms of what is so infinitely serious in this eclipse of our mission. But he admitted that it was possible that the soul of France was only slumbering; Bernanos who implores France to awaken never ceased to believe in her. She is even the only one to whom he calls out, whom he loves in her sick body, despite and beyond the invectives. His hope was invincible."[17]

As a result, Bernanos refused to join in the rising extreme-rightist chorus. In a letter dated July 2, 1934, six months after the February insurrectionist attempt, he wrote to a friend: "I am not marching with the troops of February 6. Where are they going? It strikes me that the movement, sparked by the clique of Chiappe,* manipulates a group of good people who will be used, in the end, for the supreme interest of a collapsing bourgeois society."[18] In the rioting troops and in the members of the para-military rightist organizations, Bernanos saw the dupes of the conservative forces which were manipulating them. He remembered, as I have pointed out, his own adoles-

* Paris chief of police who, although he restored order on the night of February 6, was known for his rightist sympathies. After the riots he was relieved of his duties by the government.

cent experiences among the *camelots du roi;* they too were idealists in the true French popular tradition and had been similarly exploited for interests which, at the time, he would have been unable to identify. Bernanos had the same love and compassion for the crowd which rioted in 1934 as for the Communards of 1871; it had dawned upon him years before, after the maturing period spent in the trenches of Flanders, that it had always been the same division in France between the simple people and the sagacious *bien-pensants,* and that his own place was, unequivocally, on the former's side.

In the French fascists he saw another form of dupes, less excusable than the rioting crowd because they ought to have been the country's elite. Instead, they were Machiavellians, concluding, often against their better judgment, an alliance with the bourgeois conservatives and, by the logic of this alliance, with the foreign dictators in whom the bourgeois had put their trust. For this, Bernanos could see no excuse. In the conservatives he saw miserable and dry souls, bent on preserving what was least worth it, their privileges. Bernanos took pleasure in loudly calling their bluff, but he was aware of their immense power, however fragile its foundations.

He charged the conservatives, the middle classes and the sympathizers of fascism with many sins, but underneath all, he identified a single source: the un-Christian opposition to social justice. All the rest followed from this obstinate sticking to security, property and privileges. Hatred of Blum and of the Popular Front, the glorification of Mussolini and his conquest of Abyssinia, the contempt for and undermining of the League of Nations, and finally Munich and defeat stemmed from this. Not that Bernanos necessarily took the other side and hailed the Popular Front, the League of Nations or the Spanish Republicans; but he questioned the *motives* of the bourgeoisie, the patriotic label which they fastened onto their actions, articles and conspiracies. Also, he ridiculed the "realism" which they thought was dictating their actions. He called "realistic little cads" those who scoffed at the Republic for its weaknesses while they themselves did everything in their power to weaken it and while—and Bernanos knew it—they were ready to accommodate themselves to an unfree regime and submit to the rule of force.

"REALISM" AND THE SPIRIT OF MUNICH

In an article published in November 1938 in the *Nouvelle Revue Française*, France's leading literary monthly, Julien Benda analyzed the reasons behind the absurd appeasement at Munich and the suicidal attitude of western statesmen and the western press. Why did these men yield to the dictators? asked Benda. His answer was straight and simple: out of fear of having to defeat Hitler whom they considered the bulwark, their own bulwark, against communism. In other words, it was not fear of Hitler, but fear of Hitler's enemy, who was at the same time their own enemy too: Bernanos had also reached Benda's conclusion that the French elite and middle classes had clearly chosen to ally themselves with their *national enemy* against their *class enemy*. This is how Bernanos greeted the sudden popularity of Doriot among the most respectable people and in the best salons. Doriot, as a Communist militant, had backed Abd-el-Krim's rebellion against the French: "There is not one of these stupid men and women who had not taken this boy, at the time of Abd-el-Krim, for a traitor in the pay of Moscow. And all of them are ready today to place the country's destiny in his hands if they can be persuaded that he is shrewd enough to outsmart his erstwhile friends."[19]

Naturally, Bernanos applied his conclusion about the "Machiavellism" of his "realistic" compatriots not only to Doriot but to a host of other politicians and public figures who were now selling out to France's enemies, the dictators. Benda's prediction for the future was that if a war did not come to alter the rapport of forces on the continent, the development of a hidden form of fascism was likely in France. This, Bernanos understood long before Munich. He did not pay as much attention as the intellectualist Benda to eventual institutional changes and political shifts; with a novelist's intuition he had long before felt the political climate in circles which were more or less closed to the Jewish Benda, a climate increasingly favorable to a reckless course.

THE DICTATORS

He marked, one after the other, the phases of this course. If a beginning can at all be set to it, it is the adulation with which conservative-rightist circles began to surround Mussolini. The Duce was the first dictator of stature; he had been a socialist, that is a man who was acquainted with the strategy against which he was supposed to protect the middle classes. In fact, his blackshirts had done just that in the early post-war years when the industrial areas in the North were threatened and invaded by Communist-organized work-brigades. When he turned towards the Mediterranean the French Right applauded, for it meant the humiliation of the British navy. In Abyssinia, the Duce demonstrated his courage by again challenging Great Britain and his dynamism by launching an imperial venture. He was also clever enough to respond to the aspirations of the French Right and to encourage Pierre Laval with whom he was working on an alliance to bar Germany's access to Southern Europe.

Italian propaganda thus found a ready terrain in France. Fascist funds were freely flowing into French publications willing to coöperate. Bernanos reports that one of his best friends, Robert Vallery-Radot, also received such funds with which to buy Coty's second paper, *L'Ami du Peuple*. A French press favorable to him was of course a great asset to Mussolini before and during the Abyssinian campaign, because his interest was to sow discord into the Franco-British alliance and at the League of Nations. Once again, this press was willing to identify the Duce's campaign with the "defense of the West." In fact, a manifesto bearing this title was published at the time by rightist intellectuals; and, supporting them, Henri Béraud wrote his famous article in *Gringoire*, "Why I hate the English?" Even Maurras accepted Mussolini's money. As Bernanos charged: "In 1933, M. Charles Maurras joined the party of the *bien pensant*. This great man, for whose decline and misfortune I shall always have the greatest commiseration, found himself before the painful alternative of seeing his paper perish or following the road already taken by nearly all leaders of the nationalist and clericalist press—that is taking his share, more or less directly, from the inexhaustible funds of Mussolinian propaganda."[20]

In *Les Grands Cimetières sous la lune*, and in his subsequent writings and speeches before and during World War II, Bernanos attacked Mussolini violently. His concept of warfare had a knightly stamp on it, and he felt an irrepressible revulsion before Italian tanks charging barefooted Abyssinian troops and Italian airplanes throwing incendiary bombs on thatched-roofed huts and their inhabitants. He was exasperated at reading in the pro-fascist French papers reports about "Italy carrying out a civilizing mission in Abyssinia," and about Italian bishops blessing the embarking troops. Has western Christian humanity sunk to the level of organizing massacres against miserable Negroes? he asked. Was this the task for which the elites were training themselves? When, in an interview, Mussolini's pilot son gave an enthusiastic description of his esthetic pleasure at the sight of the burning villages below his squadron, Bernanos understood that for such sins the punishment may not be late in coming.

He saw in the dictators what the fifth-century Christians had seen in Attila, the scourge of God, the executors of the punishment. It was not hard for him to realize that the admiration with which the French bourgeoisie surrounded Hitler, Mussolini and Franco was not the incense burned on the altar of chivalry and heroism in a materialistic age, but again, the expression of deadly panic before the rise of the poor. He knew that the dictators were not Christian knights, renewing the tradition of Joan of Arc, but brutal gladiators whom an effeminate society pays to whip its rebelling slaves, and to whose whips the slave-keepers themselves sooner or later submit. "Society gets along well with its poor," he wrote in *Les Grands Cimetières sous la lune*, "as long as it can absorb the malcontents in hospitals or in prisons. But when the proportion of the malcontents increases to a point of danger, society calls in its gendarmes and opens wide its graveyards."[21]

The rise of dictators is thus an indication not of a society's power, but of its weakness and abdication. It is grotesque to see for the past ten years . . . ," he wrote in 1943, "leaders of industry, officers, aristocrats, churchmen, proclaim the necessity of dictatorships, when by this they proclaim their own impotence . . . Throughout history, dictatorship has always been a powerful and clumsy instrument, made for the masses. . . . What our degenerate elites expect of a dictatorship is that it might assume the risks of leadership in their place, while it will let them take its prestige and profit."[22]

Historically and morally, dictatorships are then a period of humiliation and impotent rage; socially, they are symptoms of confusion and sickness; but Bernanos was most concerned with the concrete case his country was facing and to the predictable consequences of which it had chosen to close its eyes: the fact that under the cover of friendship with Mussolini, the French nation was subtly prepared to accept Hitler's tutelage. "Teutonic paganism would have made us distrustful; the resurrected paganism of ancient Rome seduced our humanistic traditions."[23]

There were many reasons why Hitler, and not Mussolini, was to benefit ultimately from the panic of the French middle classes and from the surrender of their elite. Theoretically, it would have been quite difficult to overcome French resistance to a man like the German dictator In addition to the traditional hatred for the *boche* which animated the middle classes be- tween 1871 and 1914, there was the obvious interest of the country in maintaining the stipulations of the Versailles treaty and in reaffirming French protection of the Eastern European nations (Poland, Czechoslovakia, Rumania and Yugoslavia) against Hitler's reactivated Germany. Even the realists could not deny this. Yet, as Bernanos remarked, there was a system- atic campaign in the French press after the mid-thirties against the Versailles treaty and its embodiment, the League of Na- tions, and also against alliance with the small powers of Eastern and Central Europe. The latter, although they had historical ties many times renewed with France and French culture, were spoken of in the press as some faraway, strange and bar- baric lands, beyond the frontiers of civilization, not worth fighting for. "To die for Dantzig? Never!" declared Marcel Déat on the eve of the war. And a British Foreign Office official describes in his recently published memoirs how Daladier seemed almost eager to sign away Czech independence at Munich.

But it is even more astonishing to find Hitler praised and ad- mired in Maurrassian circles, in direct contradiction to the spirit of Maurrassian doctrine. For Maurras, the term "Ger- manic" denoted confusion and obscurity, the very opposite of the logical Latin; he insisted on seeing in Protestantism a product of the impenetrable German forests beyond the Rhine, that is, beyond the clearly drawn lines of the Roman legions. If anything, his followers ought to have regarded the *myth* pro- pounded by Hitler as a manifestation of ancient Germania's monstrous divinities, and the *ethos* of Rosenberg and Goebbels as a third-rate concoction of pagan, Christian and romantic elements, all of which were abhorrent to the classical-Mediter- ranean mind of their mentor.

Yet, every act of Hitler was welcomed as if it had not meant the encirclement and isolation of France, a pressure on France's allies, a step towards rapprochement with Mussolini and the latter's detachment from the western powers, France and Great Britain. The occupation of the Rhineland, the return of Saar to Germany, the implantation of Nazi power across France's southern borders, in Franco's Spain, the annexation of Austria and the Sudetenland, of Czechoslovakia itself, did not alarm the nationalist-conservative circles, because everything was better than war which would "profit only the Moscow crew." And the "Moscow crew" meant not only the masters of the Kremlin, but the French workers with their demands for higher wages. Bernanos summed up the climate of opinion correctly when he wrote: "Rather Hitler than Blum! This was the slogan that Goebbels' agents were whispering into the ears of thousands of bourgeois for whom it meant: rather Hitler than such costly social reforms."[24]

Bernanos' literary activity, as I have mentioned, is circumscribed by two dates, 1926 and 1936. *The Diary of a Country Priest,* his greatest work and probably the guarantee of his literary survival, dates from the latter year, after which he never again wrote a page of fiction. Until his death, twelve years later, he published only polemical works—political, social and even politico-philosophical criticism. Not that he liked it that way; in an interview given a few months before his death, he asserted: "I am neither a polemicist, nor a pamphletist. A doctrinaire even less. God knows the sorrow I feel for no longer writing novels. This is a very great sacrifice for me. But I want, I want very much, to try to revive in people the reflexes of good faith and sincerity."[25] And, finally, on his deathbed, he said in a conversation with abbé Pézeril: "Do people imagine that if I had not attached a great importance to my polemical activity, I, a novelist, would have sacrificed my novels to it?"

It is interesting to note that Bernanos is not alone in thus paying a painful homage to the prevalence of politics in our century. Mauriac too has sacrificed his literary career—although it had reached a climax with the Nobel Prize—to weekly commentaries on the French and the world situation, to a passionate participation in the agitation of the market place. Other major French writers have faced the same choice: Péguy, Roman Rolland, Gide and Sartre have hesitated between the fictional and the polemical forms, and have, to a degree at least, sacrificed the first to the second.

However similar these choices, the motive for each is, of course, different, and for Bernanos it can be found only in what he called "vocation." This is how he tried to explain, in connection with a remark of Albert Béguin, his commitment to the nonfictional form: "The métier I have been engaged in for the past two years is not really mine, and I have never expected it to bring satisfaction to my *amour-propre*, nor any other kind of comfort. This is what the dear Albert Béguin ought to understand when he blames me for not writing novels. Oh, no doubt, he is perhaps right to think that I am made for writing novels; but, alas! every man is right also to believe that he is made for happiness. . . . Vocation is a risk, it is even the main risk of life itself. Very well, one should know how to take one's risk in such and such decisive circumstances. Vocation means *vocatus*; God calls us, nothing is truer than this. God calls us but we do not always know from where. . . . At the point where I am now, it would pain me if people thought that I have illusions left about the importance of my writings. I have said many times that I was not a writer. I belong, with all my being, with all my fibres, to an old sacerdotal civilization, to a civilization of peasants and soldiers, who have never taken this kind of people too seriously. . . . But even if I believed that the novels which I shall never write would have been as good as the dear Béguin imagines in his friendship for me, I would still not worry. Books are like men; they may get killed in war. And we are in war. We are more than ever in war."[26]

There is no reason to believe that Bernanos thought any different in 1936 than in 1947 when he wrote these lines. His choice, with *Les Grands Cimetières de la lune*, was obviously dictated by an imperative desire to find a means more direct than literature to talk to his countrymen about this "war." He felt that it was the greatest treason he had so far witnessed, a treason and a scandal so immense that continuing the novelist's trade would have seemed to him a frivolous and dishonest course of action.

His interest in the Spanish Civil War was many-sided. I have said that he and his family left the South of France in 1934 to move to Majorca because it was an inexpensive place and ideal for a man who never liked the hustle and bustle of big city life and who wanted to write in peace. In addition, the Baleares are Spanish, and Bernanos always cherished his Hispanic ancestry. He was a Frenchman and immensely, mystically proud of it; but he also belonged to the Latin race, at home near the Mediterranean no matter where and flattered by his Spanish blood and temperament. He felt kinship also with the Spanish quality of religious faith, the total commitment to militancy in Christ's ranks, the all-or-nothing pride of the Spanish soul impregnated with service and sacrifice to God and King.

Moreover, as Professor Amoroso Lima believes, Bernanos thought of Spain and Iberia during these years as the arm of God in a world gradually turning away from the divine. He had all but despaired of the France of the thirties and imagined that General Franco's rebellion, with all the aura and audacity of military glory, would be the long-expected knightly combat against the totalitarian legions of the communist and fascist antiChrist. In the first days of the Franquist revolt, the eldest of

Bernanos' sons joined the Falangists; it is not difficult to see in this young enthusiasm the paternal inspiration. Who knows if his son's departure did not prompt Bernanos to include Olivier de Sommerange's episode in his book then in the making.

His son's fighting in the ranks of the Falange, that is, the good war instead of the treacherous one that he had had to fight in 1914, is only one way of measuring the enthusiasm of Bernanos for the Spanish generals' difficult exploit. We know how Bernanos felt during the first months of the war from the seven or eight articles he sent to the weekly magazine *Sept*, a Dominican publication in Paris.

For a few weeks after the Franquist rebellion broke out, he believed that he was witnessing *gesta Dei per Hispanos*, God's intervention in the affairs of men when things were going badly. That the Spaniards were called upon to deal the death-blow against the united forces of materialism and hypocrisy must have filled him with satisfaction and compensated him, in part, for the passiveness of his own French. More than once he referred in his letters to the Spaniards as still being the people they had been in the Middle Ages, that is, still capable of genuine feelings and reactions, while the French had become inescapably dry in their bourgeois ways. Franco seemed to pay God the ransom for their cynicism—and for Mussolini's ignominy—one Latin sister-nation doing penance for the others' sins.

In August he still praised the Spaniards for their determination to "assure the moral and religious unity of the country, with iron and fire if necessary." In the rebel generals, Franco, Queipo and Yagüe, he saw soldiers of the traditional type, quick, active, accomplishing the revolution with a few strokes. But this tone disappeared very soon and his earlier confidence only made the awakening harder. Although later he wrote that he "needed ten months [July 1936—spring 1937] to discover, bit by bit, how terror functions,"[27] his notes to friends and articles in *Sept* show that he had a sharper view before that time. It must be said that for many politicians, experts and political commentators it has taken longer than ten months to realize how terror functioned, to realize that it was terror and, finally, that it was terror on both sides. Bernanos' early recognition of what the war really was came out of the inevitable comparisons between his country and Spain; he knew the number and names of people—on the Left and on the Right—who were waiting to play the same roles in such a conflict in France. As for Majorca, there the conditions of violence and the procedures of civil war existed almost in an ideal laboratory atmosphere.

"In the course of the last two years [1935–1936] . . . I found myself on the world's most favorable point for making certain observations,"[28] he noted in *Les Grands Cimetières sous la lune*. In a letter (August 27, 1936) he had written: "I am grateful to the Lord for allowing me to observe a kind of general rehearsal of the universal revolution. . . . What a chapter I could now append to my *Grand Peur!*" It was to be more than a chapter; he made it clear in his letters to friends in Paris that he had been keeping a diary which he intended to publish, only detached parts of which he sent along for printing in *Sept*. The writer-reporter's understandable joy to be present at such important events is mixed with his growing indignation. As early as September 10, he wrote that it was a remarkable experience to watch the realities of a revolution, the dirty work by the *bien-pensant* elements of the islands. Three months later he noted: "Now the hyenas appear on the scene. What follows is not for people like you and me . . . A counter-revolution is not at all what the idiots think it is, back in France." And at the beginning of 1937: "You have no idea of what is going on here. It is like a nightmare from which I cannot tear myself away . . . I am witnessing a revolution made by the military and the clericalists. It is a disgusting spectacle and it would be hard to imagine so paradoxical a mixture of cynicism and hypocricy."[29]

What struck Bernanos most and filled him with a true horror, was the role of the clergy in the civil war. In summing up Bernanos' attitude towards the Church, Father Duployé wrote that "his basic mistake is in conceiving the Church exclusively on the prophetic model and, as a result, in dreaming of a chimerical existence for it which leads him to misunderstand the conditions of its real existence."[30]

Bernanos' relationship to the clergy, high and low, is of course one of the most controversial points in his whole life and career both as a novelist and as a social critic. But Bernanos himself seems to have answered Father Duployé when he wrote in Les Grands Cimetières: "I do not think that the Church is capable of reforming itself on the human level, at least not in the sense in which Luther and Lamennais meant it. I do not desire that the Church should be perfect, since it is alive. Like the humblest and poorest of its children, the Church goes on, groping and stumbling, from this world to the next; it makes mistakes and it expiates them; but whoever wishes to turn his eyes away for a moment from its pomp and splendor, hears it sob and pray, with the rest of us, in the darkness."[31]

If Bernanos did not expect perfection from the clergy, he did, nevertheless, hope for a more impartial attitude, dictated not by the worldly interests of the Church, but in the spirit of the gospels. I have mentioned how scandalized he was by apostolic blessings being bestowed on Italian troops and planes involved not in a just war but in a last-minute colonial venture to flatter the imperial ambition of a corrupt fascism. But in Spain there was not even the excuse of a national enterprise: it was a civil war, brother against brother, in which Bernanos expected the clergy—as he always expected the elite—to show itself as father, conciliator, healer. Instead, he saw the clergy and hierarchy take off and settle down unequivocally in Franco's camp which, in Bernanos' judgment, was the camp of the military, the conservative and the bourgeois. This, in itself, would have been sufficient proof for him that the Spanish Church was guilty.

Bernanos always had a feeling of mixed contempt and ridicule for right-wing apostles who insisted that the nation was behind them and loved them, but was prevented by the demagogues and false teachers from showing its true loyalty. He saw the Spanish situation in the same light, Franco and the *bien-pensants*—civil and ecclesiastic—around him were trying to impose their rule on a nation perhaps indifferent or even hostile to its republican government, but certainly not in favor of the Franquist clique and the Falange either. Hence, in his eyes, the crusading character of the rebellion was nothing but an impudence to which the clergy had willingly lent its support. "Naive as the rightists have always been, powerful as their instinct is for unmistakably choosing unpopular causes and men, they will perhaps grant me that the Spanish war has lost its character of an explosion of national and Christian sentiments."[32]

These words, of course, as well as the whole book, were addressed to his own countrymen. On both sides of the barricade, the French were intently watching the war's outcome; many of them were by then fighting either in the Franquist or in the Republican camp. He saw the destiny of his country rehearsed before his spectator's eyes and described the mechanism of terror and persecution that France was to experience in her own body a few years later.

To begin with, he witnessed the unexpected arrival of Italian units which, in collaboration with local Falangists, set themselves the task of "cleaning up" the islands. "I saw there, at Majorca, trucks pass on the Rambla, trucks full of men. They were rolling with the noise of thunder, past the many-colored terraces which were freshly washed, in the merry expectation of the fiesta. The trucks were gray with the dust of the roads, and gray were too the men sitting in rows of four, their gray caps astray on their heads, and their hands on their trousers like well-behaved schoolboys. Every night they were picked up in distant farms, as they were returning from the fields; now they were leaving for their last journey, with shirts glued to their perspiring shoulders, their arms still heavy with the day's work, leaving the evening's soup on the table and a wife who arrived too late to the garden gate, out of breath, pressing a small package: A Dios! recuerdos!"[33]

Who were the "purgers" of Majorca? The island was a small world, easily observed. Bernanos, powerless in his rage and compassion, horror-struck by a manifestation of evil more inexorable than he had ever known, walked the streets, listened at the cafés, at the barbershop, to neighbors. He heard silence, the silence of churchyards, descend on the gay little villages, and whispering fear steal among the houses, among friends. Purge committees were set up, consisting of "the bourgeois landowner, the sexton, the curate's housekeeper, some right-thinking farmers with their wives, finally some youngsters hastily recruited by the Falange, converted since yesterday, impatient to give guarantees of good conduct."[34]

Meanwhile, those who were the possible objects of the purge, lived in terror. "I saw at Majorca," Bernanos wrote later, in *La France contre les Robots*, "during Holy Week in 1936, while teams of purgers visited the villages and liquidated the wrong-thinking, the terrorized population crowd to the holy tables in order to obtain the invaluable certificate of Easter communion."[35]

Thus the greatest scandal in all this, for Bernanos, was the confusion of Christianity with order. If any means used against communism or suspected communism is legitimate or even Christian, then the champions of Christ will be the masters of totalitarian regimes, Hitler, Mussolini or the Mikado. How could the clergy accept such an ambiguous position? How can the priests be shocked by the anti-clericalism of the Spanish people when they themselves confuse the social order with order in the streets and acclaim the first military who flaunts the former and secures the latter? Granted, peace and order are important; it is just, wrote Bernanos, addressing the hierarchy, that "Your Eminences recognize the right of legitimate defense to the proprietor whom his workers come to besiege in his house. But do Your Eminences recognize the same right to the workers who wish to protect their families against hunger?"

The central point of *Les Grands Cimetières sous la lune* was telling the truth about Majorca, about the civil war and also the planned suicide of nations at the hands of false elites and dictators; ultimately, however, the point was the truth about the scandal of Christendom. If six thousand priests were massacred by the Spanish Reds, wrote Bernanos in *Scandale de la Vérité*, there were assassinated as many peasants in Majorca alone. Christians cannot rest until light is shed on the acts of priests who encouraged such killings. He kept asking if the old Pope Pius XI knew what was going on, if the "refined Monsignori," if the Archbishop of Palma, if the "clericalist party" were to go unpunished for being "the sly intermediaries of the evil rich." No justification for the alliance with Franco can be accepted under the pretext that between two evils the General was the one with whom it was possible to come to an agreement, whom one may control. Such an agreement would only lead to a definitive estrangement of the people from the Church and Christianity. The Church will, of course, try later to pass on responsibility for the atrocities to someone else, possibly to Franco himself; but the events that Bernanos witnessed were too obvious for anybody to forget.[36]

Bernanos put such a value on his work about Majorca, that when the manuscript disappeared in the rush of moving back to France, he decided at once to compose its 350 pages again. The reception of the book, as could be expected, was far from unanimously favorable: there was a very enthusiastic and a very indignant reaction. Bernanos always cherished the letter of a highly placed Roman prelate who sent him his blessing for having written the book, and let him understand that it was read by the Pope himself.[37] Those, however, whom *Les Grands Cimetières* so vehemently attacked could not forgive him. General Franco, at the threshold of victory when the book appeared, was the uncontested hero of the French Right; and the government which had not dared, not even under the socialist Léon Blum, to help the Republicans openly was soon to send old Marshal Pétain as ambassador to Burgos, Franco's headquarters.

Bernanos himself described the reception he and his words received when he returned from Majorca with news of the scandal perpetrated there. First, he spoke of the political climate he found as he set foot in France and began to talk with people: "After three years abroad, I found my country profoundly divided against itself. I literally did not recognize it. The spring of 1937 has no doubt been one of the most tragic springs of France, a spring of civil war. What used to be political rivalry, now became social hatred in an intolerable atmosphere of reciprocal fright. Fear! Fear! Fear! It was the spring of Fear. The forces of life must be very powerful if the chestnut trees bore their flowers even in this stifling air. I did not recognize my friends' faces. 'This must end, and right away!' peaceful folks were stammering."[38] We must understand at this point that Bernanos still had the illusion of playing a providential role. He thought he returned from Majorca with a warning which, in the mouth of a celebrated writer who had never hidden his rightist convictions, would be listened to, even in influential circles. He believed that his countrymen were, after all, famous for their Cartesian logic, that they understood ideas which were clearly and distinctly exposed to them, supported by facts, by an eye-witness' account. No matter how the sanguine Spaniards were carried away in their fratricidal passion, Frenchmen would understand the language of national interest when Italian and German troops were fighting south of the Pyrénées, and enemy submarines were criss-crossing the Mediterranean. Further, on the Baleares, Bernanos had little personal con-

tact with France. Occasionally, some friends would come to
visit him from the mainland, as when de Jouvenel and Drieu
came to urge him to join Doriot's new party. But ordinarily he
read only the newspapers which either did not commit themselves too far on account of the explosiveness of the international situation, or affected a strict neutrality out of fear
of upsetting Hitler's and Mussolini's plans.

"I had nothing to tell the men of the Left," Bernanos begins
his account; "I came to talk to the men of the Right. I thought
at first that this would be easy. I also thought they were not
well-informed. It turned out that they knew as much as I.—
They said to me: 'Italians in Spain? So much the better! There
ought to be more of them!—Germans too? Perfect.—Sum-
mary executions? Excellent! No sentimentality, please.—But
your papers, I said, which . . . Our papers say what they
must say. You are not going to bring *that* up, are you? You are
not going to play the game of M. Jouhaux [leader of the
C.G.T. labor union]? Imagine that a construction worker at
the World Fair is paid more than a hundred francs a day! Yes,
sir!' "[39]

Bernanos admits that he was left speechless at this outburst
of bitterness. What could he have replied? Bernanos now understood that his friends, who were, for the most part, when the
chips were down, representative members of the conservative
bourgeoisie, had chosen fascism as a protection. Not fascism in
its ferocious demagogic ways, but as a shield of respectable
men against the masses and their demands. But he also understood that they were dupes in believing that the dictators would
faithfully hold this shield in front of them, would sacrifice
themselves in the defense of the bourgeois values and interests.

They were dupes, for they overlooked the fact that, in
their own way, the "reactionary" dictators were representatives of the masses, and that the masses were holding them in
bondage exactly as much as they imposed, in turn, their will
upon the people. "Fascism and Hitlerism," Bernanos wrote in

Les Grands Cimetières, addressing his friends, "propose to you models of revolution. I doubt that you could profit by them as they do not seem to serve the interests of your class, its habits and prejudices. Mussolini and Hitler are what they are, but they are not your men. Between us, they hardly like you. I do not think that certain of your social attitudes appeal to them, that they would permit, for example, the corner grocer to keep raising the price of his merchandise while he condemns the principle of proportionate increase of salaries and wages. I doubt that they would let you play against the franc at the stockmarket, while you order M. Jouhaux to encourage the spirit of patriotic sacrifice among his troops . . . But suppose that you are still willing to support some sort of a [fascist] revolution. What model would you choose? I have just seen the kind of revolution which is most dangerous for you, the kind to which you would say, with your usual reaction before certain things, 'there are things one does not do.' Well, the revolution I have seen is one of those. The world will not accept a clerical, bourgeois, or military terror. It may be justified, in your eyes, by the threat of the other terror; but we are not speaking here of morals, we are speaking of history; there is a fatality here on which you will suffer shipwreck."[49]

Of all those whom Bernanos attacked in connection with the Majorcan atrocities, there was only one individual mentioned, the Archbishop of Palma. As the head of the Church on the Baleares, he incurred Bernanos' special wrath for not disassociating his clergy from the many acts of terror and vengeance, and for openly favoring the particularly brutal Italian intervention. Repeatedly, in the pages of *Les Grands Cimetières* and in subsequent writings, Bernanos mentioned the Archbishop of Palma as the epitome of the evil Churchman, the twentieth-century counterpart of Cauchon and the other inquisitors who interrogated, betrayed, and condemned Joan of Arc. During the second World War, every time Bernanos pronounced a moral indictment of the prelates who collaborated with Vichy, he mentioned this personage as their prototype.

The Archbishop's reaction to this treatment in *Les Grands Cimetières* was expressed in a letter sent to *l'Action Française*. In September 1938 the Archbishop, Joseph Miralles Sbert, wrote a letter to the nationalist paper denouncing the book as containing grave calumnies about Spain and ideas which could rightly come under suspicion from the point of view of the faith. He further accused the author of having encouraged his son's membership in the Falange for the purpose of obtaining confidential information concerning the movement.

At the time of the writing Bernanos was no longer in France. In July of that year he had left with his family for Brazil, sick, as he wrote, of his country's humiliation and of the alarming rise of cynical willingness to let the dictators prevail in Europe. We have seen that quite early in his youth, years before the first World War, the idea of emigration to South America had been popular among the friends of Bernanos. His decision to leave France and the European continent a year after his return from Majorca had obviously to do with his disgust with the developing situation of which the Spanish Civil War gave only a foretaste, but also with the old dream of living in a semi-savage land, engaged in farm work, and with people close to nature for neighbors. Already in a letter of July 1934 he had mentioned his hope of leaving for Paraguay.

His departure was, nevertheless, interpreted as a sign of sur-render, and, after the outbreak of the second World War, as the cowardice of a man leaving the sinking boat. Archbishop Miralles Sbert's letter was a good pretext for *l'Action Française* to deliver a belated *coup de grâce* now, years after the con-troversy over the *Figaro* collaboration. Maurras' paper asked, in fact, whether Bernanos was not a sort of unofficial messenger of French Christian democratic circles sent to Brazil in order to encourage similar elements there in their opposition to au-thoritarian tendencies manifest in Brazilian political life. Those who knew of Bernanos' lifelong dislike of Christian democratic and Christian socialist movements—in which he saw "stragglers of Marxism"—could see the direction of the thrust delivered by the *l'Action Française*. For the Maurrassian organ, Bernanos had simply ceased to be a "man of the Right"; his every action and word were now subject to question and suspicion.

Not all of the responses to Bernanos' great work were hostile. Throughout his later travels, in South America, then in France and Tunisia, Bernanos kept as a precious souvenir the letter Simone Weil had written to him after reading *Les Grands Cimetières sous la lune*. Simone Weil was Jewish, a brilliant Sorbonne graduate and a communist sympathizer before the Spanish Civil War. In harmony with her uncompromising solidarity with the French working class, she left her lycée teaching at the news of the Spanish events in the summer of 1936 and went to Spain in order to fight in defense of the government. The experiences and the reaction of this typical Leftist intellectual closely paralleled those of Bernanos: the brutality and murder in the leftist ranks scandalized her in the same way as Bernanos was scandalized by the rightist-clerical atrocities; the gratuitous, sadistic execution of Catholic priests horrified Simone Weil in exactly the same measure as the nightly trips of the Franquist-fascist trucks horrified Bernanos.[41] It is moving to see how these two human beings whom everything separated—age, faith, intellectual background, world outlook—were absolutely of one mind in their denunciation of injustice. This is what the Marxist intellectual-militant wrote to the Catholic royalist: "The war in Spain was not, as it had appeared to me at the start, a war waged by famished peasants against landowners, and their ecclesiastic accomplices, but it was a war between Russia, Germany and Italy. . . . I do not see anybody, outside of yourself alone, who, to my knowledge, has been immersed in the atmosphere of this war and could resist it. What does it matter to me that you are a royalist, a disciple of Drumont? You are incomparably closer to me than my comrades from the Aragon militia—the comrades whom I used to love."[42]

NOTES

1. *La Droite en France*, p. 216.
2. Quoted by Julien Benda in "Les Démocraties bourgeoises et l'Allemagne," in *Nouvelle Revue Française*, November 1938. Translated by J. Robert Loy in *From the N.R.F.*, edited by Justin O'Brien (New York: Farrar Straus and Cudahy, 1958), p. 360.
3. Ernst von Salomon, *Fragebogen* (New York: Doubleday, 1955), p. 238.
4. Quoted by Pierre Andreu, *Drieu, témoin et visionnaire* (Grasset, 1956).
5. Jose María Gironella, *The Cypresses Believe in God* (New York: Alfred Knopf, 1956), pp. 446, 456.
6. *Maurras et son temps*, I, pp. 270–71.
7. *Ibid.*, II, p. 116.
8. Alfred Fabre-Luce, *Le Siècle prend figure* (Flammarion, 1949), p. 217.
9. P. 71.
10. *La France contre les Robots*, pp. 112–17.
11. *Nous autres, Français*, p. 244.
12. *Diary of a Country Priest*, p. 303.
13. Drieu la Rochelle, *Mesure de la France*
14. Montherlant, *Le Maître de Santiago*
15. Reported among the reminiscences of Maurice Colrat.
16. Quoted by H. Urs von Balthasar in *Le Chrétien Bernanos*, p. 68.
17. "Le désespoir de Drieu La Rochelle," *Le Figaro Litteraire*, July, 1953.
18. *Bulletin*, Nos. 2–3, March 1950.
19. *Les Grands Cimetières sous la lune*, p. 59.

20. From an article on Péguy, 1943. Reproduced in *Bulletin* No. 10, June 1952.
21. *Les Grands Cimetières sous la lune*, p. 202.
22. *Lettre aux Anglais*, p. 76.
23. From an article written in Brazil, 1940. (*Bulletin* No. 27, July 1956.)
24. *Le Chemin de la Croix-des-Ames*, p. 118.
25. Interview in Combat, March 20, 1948.
26. "Nous sommes en guerre," *Carrefour*, July 16, 1947.
27. *Les Grands Cimetières sous la lune*, p. 123.
28. *Ibid.*, p. 86.
29. Letters dated December 12 and 28, 1936; January 18, 1937. The articles, which were first received by friends, then forwarded to Father Boisselot, the editor of *Sept*, were accompanied with short notes in which Bernanos commented on the events he was witnessing. There is, incidentally, no difference between what he wrote in the articles and in the letters; he expressed his views in both sincerely and with courage. In this way we may trust our reading of his rapid change of mind which occurred between July 1936 and the end of that year.
30. *In La Vie Intellectuelle*, quoted by Ernst Erich Noth, "The Prophetism of Georges Bernanos," Yale French Studies.
31. *Les Grands Cimetières sous la lune*, pp. 114–15.
32. *Ibid.*, p. 87.
33. *Ibid.*, pp. 72–3.
34. *Ibid.*, p. 125.
35. *La France contre les Robots*, pp. 45–6.
36. "The Spanish experience was, perhaps, the capital event of my life . . . It gave me a chance to observe to what depth the totalitarian poison had corrupted the conscience of Catholics and even that of priests." "Autobiographie," *La Nef*, August, 1948.
37. Bernanos, as he reports in the "Autobiographie," seems to have had knowledge that *Les Grands Cimetières* would have been put on the Index without the express opposition of Pius XI.
38. *Les Grands Cimetières sous la lune*, pp. 116–17.
39. *Ibid.*, pp. 118–19.
40. *Ibid.*
41. Simone Weil proved her courage by trying to cover, with her

own body, a priest whom her comrades were about to execute. On her insistence they finally pretended to let the priest go, only to shoot him down a few minutes later.

42. *Bulletin,* No. 4, June, 1950.

5 Vichy: "A Ballet Danced in a Graveyard"

It is reported of Maurras that when he heard of the defeat of the French Army in 1940 and the decision to ask for an armistice, he exclaimed: "What a divine surprise!" It goes without saying that the leader of the *Action Française* was rejoicing, not at the defeat of his country, but at what seemed in the eyes of many patriots the same thing, the opportunity to build new institutions on the ruins of the old, republican ones. The price for this undertaking appeared, of course, rather high; but, as Bernanos remarked in *Nous autres, Français,* Maurras had hoped, since the success of Franco's rebellion, that the King would soon return to the French throne, if necessary, with the help of foreign intervention. After all, Louis XVIII had returned to Paris, after the fall of Napoleon, between rows of foreign bayonets.

Maurras' exclamation was a symptom of the critical state of France as noted by Bernanos upon his return from Majorca. The bourgeoisie was showing a new aggresiveness; in the last three years before the outbreak of the war there developed an almost open warfare between the Right and the Left. In June 1936 an unexpected sit-down strike had forced the bourgeois parties in the National Assembly to yield to Léon Blum and soon to the Popular Front. But, realizing their own weakness and frightened by the workers' demands—encouraged also by

the Blum government's timidity at home and in its relationship
to the Spanish Civil War—the industrialists at once began to
organize and offer open support to the Right. The so-called
Matignon Agreement regarding the forty-hour week, paid
vacations and wage raises was soon repudiated by the employers, and the country began drifting fatefully towards a
state of paralysis, lagging production and inflation.

Little wonder that under these circumstances substantial seg-
ments of the population put their trust in a drastic solution. If a
Maurras impatiently expected the breakdown of the democratic Republic, it is only normal that his feelings were reflected
in the attitude of various other circles. Bernanos, who always
indicted the elites first, spoke of "defeatism" among army
officers who "hated the Republic more than they loved
France." "There was, there has always been, a faction favoring
the armistice, favoring renunciation, resignation, and this
faction was not recruited from among the ignorant masses of
our people. . . . It was recruited from among the elites . . .
The best educated, the most distinguished army officers, the
aristocratic and the *bien-pensant* elements in the Navy, spoke
out spontaneously, passionately, angrily in favor of peace at
any price."[1]

The middle classes, naturally, followed suit since for them
one thing alone mattered: to be saved from the Left and from
social upheavals. Who cared if for this purpose the pro-fascist
elite was willing to sell the independence of the nation? " 'Perhaps they *have* sold out. But, after all, they are defending us
against the Reds' . . . The bourgeoisie openly boasted of
preferring injustice to disorder."[2] Those of the bourgeoisie who
possessed the necessary capital tried to leave a country in
which economics adjustments endangered their profits. Bernanos noted this too: "The labor unions are not the number one
enemy," he wrote, "the escape of capital is just as efficient a
blackmail against my country as the strikes."[3]

But what exasperated Bernanos most was to find his predictions concerning the role of the clergy materialize. Not only in Spain, but in France too it seemed to be ready to cover the shortsighted conservative interests with the cloak of religion. He had struck a particularly bitter note in *Les Grands Ci-metières*, with the French situation in mind. He compared the beginnings of the Dominican-led, thirteenth-century Inquisition with middle-class repression of the proletariat: "Like the communists today, so the heretics of the time were a threat to the faith and to the possessions of the leading classes. The latter were quick in persuading their governments that the Faith could wait but that the interests of ownership demanded more energetic measures. In such a way the Preachers ended up by supplying the personnel for a vast cleaning-up operation, similar to the one I saw functioning in Spain . . . It seems that not only the peace of the military, but social peace too must be bought every twenty years by the sacrifice of a few million people. Is it possible that the system itself is not worth the sacrifice?"[4]

The declaration of war in 1939 by which a reluctant France found herself again at the side of her equally reluctant ally, Great Britain, far from extinguishing the fire of such domestic strife, exacerbated the already violent passions; as General de Gaulle writes in the first volume of his *Mémoires*, in the spring of 1940, "certain circles insisted on seeing the enemy in Stalin rather than in Hitler . . . They were more preoc-cupied with finding a means to fight Russia [by declaring war alongside Finland] than in carrying on the combat against the Reich."[5]

Thus Maurras and his disciples were not alone in their agree-able surprise when Hitler's rapidly advancing armies brought the latent antagonism within the body of the nation into a sharp focus; large sections of parliament and public opinion agreed that the defeat would be a kind of divine retribution for the corruption of French politicians and public figures throughout the course of the Third Republic. The vengeance postponed after 1918 could now be revived and brought down fully on the heads of those who were held responsible for France's decadence. Among these were Blum, Daladier, Gamelin and Mandel—that is, the representative statesmen and military men of the period, later formally indicted by Vichy— and even André Gide whose influence on French youth was held pernicious and immoral.

From the moment that the Germans broke through the Meuse-line, writes Alfred Fabre-Luce, a follower of Doriot's *Parti Populaire Français*, "many Frenchmen decided in full consciousness to rally to Hitlerism . . . That night, May 16, 1940, they finally became convinced that the unity of Europe was accomplished, and they dared feel happy about it."[6]

One would imagine that the Army fell into a state of despair as it was obliged to yield, often for lack of tanks, planes, or even ammunition, to the detested enemy. This may have been the feeling in the ranks, although the apathy of the high command had begun its demoralizing work already in the first few months of the hostilities. But in the highest military circles, there was little sign of dissatisfaction over the turn that events were taking. As General de Gaulle reports, Marshal Pétain, an old soldier who had seen many battles lost and won, took it almost as a natural course of Franco-German warfare that the two nations should alternate in defeating each other. In 1871 it was the Germans' turn, in 1918 that of France; it was only fair that the god Mars should this time show his favors on the other side of the Rhine.

But there was more involved than an old soldier's prejudice. While the confused politicians and military men were keeping an official eye on the conduct of the war, in the back of many minds there arose the anguished question: what will the defeat mean for the domestic front? What will the Left do in the chaos that the Germans might want to maintain in France while they prepared to invade the British Isles? What are the instructions of the Communist Party, outlawed and driven underground the previous September? What will happen in the capital after the government has fled to Bordeaux or, as some insisted that it should, to North Africa? Already on June 8, General Weygand gave voice to these preoccupations: "Ah, if I could only be sure," he confided to de Gaulle, "that the Germans will let me keep the necessary forces to maintain order"! And he started a systematic campaign to persuade the ministers, Premier Paul Reynaud in particular, that the war was lost, that it was developing into a useless massacre of the army and of the civilian population.

His influence on the old Marshal was considerable. But other voices were also whispering into Pétain's ears. The opportunity was excellent, indeed unique, to enable him to assume the posture of savior of the country he had saved once before at Verdun. The Maurrassian school, which was well represented around him and had its adherents and sympathizers in the army as well, put the pressure on him, knowing well where his sympathies lay. The defeat was bound to be the disgrace of the Republic itself. To rebuild the land on new foundations, a new outlook, new personnel and a new order were necessary.

VICHY

The foundations of a new order were to be manufactured by the Vichy regime, the National Revolution and Marshal Pétain. Pétain himself knew next to nothing about politics and had obtained what guiding ideas he possessed from Maurras and the latter's disciple, the ex-socialist Raphael Alibert. As a soldier used to command, Pétain instinctively hated the parliamentary system and distrusted the politicians of the Third Republic. His military fame, his convictions and his recent ambassadorship to Spain made him ideally eligible for the role of a Franco; his entourage quickly persuaded him that he was also a kind of second St. Louis or Joan of Arc. From February 1934 on, a secret braintrust had begun gathering about him, hoping, incidentally, that in Pétain's new France their personal ambitions would also receive a long overdue consideration.

The beginnings of the Vichy regime were not fascistic in the sense that a new strata of the population gained a foothold through a popular party as had happened in Germany. On the contrary, the regime leaned on the support of traditional classes, the clergy, the army and the *notabilities*, and its leadership was formed, with few exceptions, by the immediately available personnel of rightist organizations like the *Croix de Feu* or the *Redressement Français*.

The first task was, as Laval indicated, "to destroy the fetishism of democracy which had delivered the nation to the worst excesses of capitalism."[7] The occupying power achieved this at one stroke. But now Frenchmen were needed, men of dedication, to accomplish the second phase: the National Revolution which was to be a reply to 1789. Perhaps the Marshal, and certainly Pierre Laval, despised the many ideologues who now avidly presented the social and political panaceas. But time was pressing; Hitler's New Order would not wait. With considerable naiveté, the principles of the National Revolution were counted upon to serve as the groundwork for a new *European* ideology.

In theory, the National Revolution rejected both capitalism and collectivism and denounced the parliamentary system as senile and unable to cope with problems arising from the new modes of production. It favored instead a corporatist state (in agreement with papal pronouncements) with a large degree of autonomy for regions and professions. It objected to the "excessive individualism" and the "ethical neutrality" that the republican-bourgeois school system inculcated in the minds of the young (and which it now tried to remedy with liberal subsidies to private, mainly Catholic schools).

The intellectuals who elaborated these doctrines did not "belong" to Vichy in the same sense as, let us say, the Communist Party has intellectuals in its camp. The Right in France usually does not form political parties, but rather leagues or committees which are loose if compared with the disciplined leftist parties. Even after the seizure of power in 1940 they did not form a party, although the out-and-out collaborators kept urging the formation of a French National Socialist party on the Nazi pattern. Then too, the occupying Germans prevented even the semblance of an articulate political life. The high-handed manner with which they treated even the most servile Vichyite collaborationists imposed upon the puppet government the necessity of *ad-hoc* decisions and secret maneuvers incompatible with sustained and coherent policy and the observance of any rule of conduct.

Principles and practices were given up in quick succession rather than imbedded in a permanent structure. As far as the personnel was concerned, teams succeeded one another with the same rapidity; the earlier idealists gave way to practical-minded men skillful at delaying tactics, and they in turn to rabid ideologues without either patriotism or Laval's supreme art in negotiating.

Their and Vichy's sinking into nihilism was a foregone conclusion. Emptied of ideals, dispirited by the failure of ideologies, they had nothing to oppose to the yawning abyss of the Teutonic *Götterdämmerung*.

After his return from Majorca, Bernanos stayed less than eighteen months in France before he left again, this time for a longer trip and a longer absence, for Brazil. Of the two books that he brought back from Majorca, *The Diary of a Country Priest* established his reputation as perhaps the greatest Catholic novelist of the century, more penetrating and more spiritual than either of his two possible rivals, Mauriac or Graham Greene. He was aware of the brilliance of his achievement; even while working on the novel, he had written to friends that "it was to be a masterpiece." The other book, *Les Grands*

Cimetières sous la lune, was also a masterpiece in its genre, a great polemical piece written with passion and indignation, with all the power of Bernanos' satire and prophetic insight. We have seen what the response to it was.

Thus, when Bernanos arrived in Brazil, in the first days of August 1938, he brought with him the reputation that his novels and controversies had generated; he was to be, during the seven years of his stay, one of France's true representatives on the distant continent, registering the love and respect that the South Americans felt for his country, and trying his best to preserve the exalted image of France in their consciousness. In this way, he was from the beginning a controversial figure put in a delicate situation. He made no secret of his opinions and freely expressed his contempt for the "spirit of Munich" dictating his country's official policy, his humiliation at the news of the armistice, his hatred for Pétain and Vichy and his support of de Gaulle and the Resistance. He continued to write—on the kitchen table of his poorly furnished farmhouse instead of the old marbletops of French provincial cafés— commenting on the mid-century world: on France's dreary present and future destiny, on his hopes for the time after the war, on the menace of dictatorship and on the more subtle tyrannies of the "robot mentality" and technology.

Professor Amoroso Lima tells of his extraordinary impression at meeting Bernanos for the first time. What struck him and the other members of the reception committee of Brazilian writers and intellectuals was the coexistence in one man of two temperaments, the "roaring lion" and the "clear-eyed child." These two temperaments are, of course, not contradictory; in Professor Lima's estimation Bernanos was always, under any circumstances, simple and forthright, capable of the most astonishing fury and, in the next minute, of mildness and lovableness, displaying the curiosity and gratefulness of a child. He gave himself, without a mask and without pretense, immediately projecting his intense interest in everything around him. While holding forth magnificently for hours, living the roles of men whom he loved, detested, valued or fought, he was also able to become absorbed in the gigantic panorama of the Brazilian hinterland and the mysterious silence of the jungle around his farm.

Bernanos had left France in bitterness. We have seen that he was, at the time, at the pinnacle of his literary success; he could have chosen to be one of the artistic lions of high society and the salons, for in the eyes of the sophisticated he was more than a brilliant writer. Like André Malraux on the "Left," Bernanos possessed the quality of political *engagement* to enhance his literary prestige. The fact that he did not care about either Left or Right would probably have made his reputation even more intriguing. But Bernanos did not long for personal glory. The success of his literary achievement had come to him when he was nearly forty years old; it never ceased to astonish him. Recognition and fame came to him like a child born to an elderly father; it is even more remarkable, therefore, that this belated but considerable success did not distract him but, on the contrary, made him even freer to remain an essentially solitary man, treading his own path.

Thus Bernanos was not an emigrant, much less a refugee; he left France because he refused to be the witness of her coming decomposition, the witness of France's road to Golgotha, the stations of which were Munich, the annexation of Czechoslovakia, the halfhearted "phony war," the surrender and the role of Pétain. In his voluntary exile, these events were further probed and dramatized in his imagination; time and distance deepened his understanding. For the first time in his life he lived in a truly foreign land and could observe directly the repercussion of European and French events in a foreign press and in the reaction of a nation so sympathetic to France yet so different. In this way he was forced to discover a new aspect of his country, the image it presents to others, and this discovery remained compellingly present to him. It filled him

with an immense pride and happiness to see how responsive his
South American hosts were to every vicissitude of France's
destiny, how they still considered France the "guide of nations," how the episodes of French history had become legends
which everybody knew and cherished.

It was even more intolerable for Bernanos to learn, then, day
by day and under the compassionate glance of his Brazilian
friends, about the phases of the defeat, the circumstances of the
surrender and the servitudes of occupation. As he had already
been away a year when the surrender took place, he could
measure how acute the country's disease was and how far it
had advanced. The Brazilians, whom he began to know and
love, became for him the representatives of the world's public
opinion, keenly aware that Europe was in the process of betraying their ideals and their dreams. In the judgment of Bernanos, for whom France was always the measure of mankind's
spiritual well-being, the greatest traitor was not Hitler's Germany, or Stalin's Russia, but France—Vichy, Pétain and the
collaborators.

They were traitors, first of all, because they were *mediocre*,
even before the war. Bernanos' violent criticism of Vichy,
reaction and fascism have to be seen in the context of this whole
period from 1918 to 1940; he indicted both Left and Right for
the final crisis of his country. In his judgment, "the days of
Munich were cruel reminders of the accursed days of 1920,
with the same ignoble selfishness and evasion."[8] And after the
war he referred derisively to Daladier and Chamberlain as the
Big Two, "big scoundrels," pompous and cowardly, as irresponsible as the Big Four later. Daladier and the politicians
of the Third Republic around him were really not much
better than Pétain's team which followed them; they had simply
wagered on the wrong horse. They had been as "realistic" as
Vichy was to be: in the concrete terms of international politics,
they had trusted the Hitlerist bulwark against the Soviet Union,
abandoned Czechoslovakia for "peace in our time," hoped

to set Mussolini against Hitler, Hitler against Stalin, and so on. But, as Bernanos firmly believed, the "realists" always end by becoming the dupes of their own self-assurance, lack of vision and courage—of their mediocrity. "Whoever has in him the making of a gullible creature, can, in his turn, become a cheat." And it was hard for him to forgive that France should be presented to the world as a land of mediocre minds and characters, petty and sly; "other nations," he wrote after his return from Brazil, "expect of Frenchmen to show themselves superior to them, to be, in fact, superior."

Again and again one must emphasize Bernanos' mystical view of France and her destiny. Hence his suffering that, during the war years, the world was deprived of France's voice, "a human voice in a world of robots;" and hence also his support of de Gaulle who came in the providential hour to incarnate this voice. His denunciation of Vichy and the collaborators was, therefore, uncompromising, as was, incidentally, the General's whose ideas were in so many respects identical to his own.

In the numerous articles that Bernanos wrote during the war, he analyzed the situation with great clarity. He believed, even while the Germans were piling victory upon victory, that the failure of Hitler and his new order was inevitable, that the entire Nazi tidal wave would break on the deep undercurrent of resistance in the old nations of Europe. German successes, spectacular and brilliant as they were, would not end in a final, conclusive victory: "Hitler may well exhaust Europe," Bernanos wrote as early as the spring of 1941, "he will be unable to organize it; every one of his victories will, on the contrary, only further disorganize the continent."[9]

Not that he underestimated Hitler's genius; writing about the German dictator, Bernanos always used the tone of reason, not that of a hysterical propagandist. He saw in Hitler not so much a phenomenon without example, an unparalleled German warlord, but a product of the Germanic soul, kept in a state of unrest by a "Christianisme manqué": "Nobody can

accuse me of having believed in the 'good Germany' of Jaurès
—the Germany of the social-democrats—or in the 'good Germany' of the Catholic Central Party—that of Mr. Sangnier. I
have always believed—even before 1914—that Germany
showed some particularly serious and acute symptoms of universal perversion . . . Germany is a Christian nation gone
wrong."[10]

This lack of a possible inner appeasement was driving the
Nazis, according to Bernanos, to new "Caesarian conquests,"
not in the military sense, but with the missionary zeal of fanatics.
Hitler's temporary advantages were due to the inherent im-
morality of all dictatorships: "Dictatorships have the immense
advantage over nations which try to live by the civilized political traditions of Europe that they are not bound by moral obligations";[11] but this advantage must be short-lived because, in
the end, dictatorships are not so efficient as they claim to be.
"The enemy keeps repeating," Bernanos said in one of his war-
time "Addresses to Frenchmen" (*Appels aux Français*), "that
the democracies are powerless before the problem of governing. But the fascistic systems do not solve these problems either,
they merely suppress them by crushing every possible reaction
of those whom they govern."[12]

Here we see the expression of one of Bernanos' favorite
ideas, that there is, in the last analysis, no qualitative difference
between the nazi-type dictatorial regimes and the bourgeois-
capitalist system. In the eyes of Bernanos, the capitalist countries
were economic dictatorships even before the rise of the strong
men. More than that, they were tyrannies also in the sense that
they began to utilize the means of modern technology with the
goal of directing their citizens' destinies. "Let me take care of
you," the bourgeois-democratic regime begins by whispering
in people's ears, and in no time it takes over the monopoly of
thinking for them. In this respect, by the way, not only fascism,
but also communism hardly differs from the western democracies: "there is no point," Bernanos said a few months before

his death, "in opposing communism and capitalism. They are the same thing. Both aim at the enormous growth of the States . . . which exploits its citizens."[13]

Resistance to fascism, then, could not come in the name of a better economic distribution because it would be ridiculous if the capitalistic regimes made such a claim. It must come from the hidden resources of the old Christian nations of Europe and, above all, from the deeply ingrained sentiments of "French liberty which will become, at the same time, the liberty of the human race . . . It is not you, dear Mr. Hitler, whom we fear most. We will manage to overcome you and your people if we manage to keep our souls intact."[14]

DE GAULLE

This is what General de Gaulle managed to do. The two elements on which he had built his difficult wartime leadership and which he trusted absolutely to carry him through the war were his insistence that no compromise must be made with Vichy and its servile personnel and his no less categorical demand that France should be recognized as a free and sovereign nation by the Allies in their dealings with him, France's sole representative.

But the Allies, especially the United States, never trusted de Gaulle. President Roosevelt simply did not understand that France needed a "mystique" to oppose Hitler's Nazi ideology and Vichy's National Revolution. Roosevelt and Churchill were charismatic leaders themselves, but they failed to recognize the same quality in the dry, obstinate, obsessed figure of de Gaulle. Consequently, Roosevelt preferred to support, one after the other, the wrong men—Pétain, Darlan, Giraud—men unacceptable not only to France, but also in the moral climate which the war generated and victory required. "It is a strategic error," de Gaulle commented, "to place oneself in a situation contradictory to the moral character of this war . . . If

France one day discovers that because of the British and Americans her liberation consists of Darlan, the Allies can perhaps win the war from a military point of view, but will lose it morally, and ultimately there will be only one victor: Stalin."[15]

In view of the General's image of France and his wartime actions as the representative of "true France," it is easy to understand why Bernanos hailed him as "the sole legitimate inheritor of Verdun's three hundred thousand dead, against an old impostor who has lost his honor."[16] Bernanos shared with de Gaulle the idea that in every crisis of the French nation there had appeared a providential figure to lead it out of its predicament: Philip Augustus, Joan of Arc, Louis XI, Louis XIV, Napoleon, Clemenceau. In this gravest of all crises, he was convinced that the General was the expected providential figure: "De Gaulle's greatness, his conformity to the rhythm of history, is that he redresses, but does not break, like Pétain, the country's destiny."[17] Naturally, he found in de Gaulle one of those rare free men who *are* the State because they are "capable of serving it and of conceiving clearly its nature, elaborating an idea of the State acceptable to all."[18]

Over against this image and this concept of France, her destiny and exalted leadership, what did Vichy offer to an attentive world? "A handful of degenerate noblemen, officers without brains and heart, intellectuals in the pay of speculators, shameless academicians, servile prelates, in short, a syndicate of rancor presided over by Marshal Pétain."[19] Encouraged in turn, by Hitler, by conservative forces at home, by the Allies themselves, this "syndicate" of Vichy "will remain in history . . . like a kind of grotesque *divertissement* in the manner of Molière: a ballet of academicians, of women of the world, of admirals and archbishops, against a bloody background, a ballet danced in a cemetery."[20]

If there is a meaning in the stereotyped expression that a man may be the conscience of a nation, Bernanos during the war years deserves this title. At a time when nearly everybody was tempted sorely to join whoever seemed victorious; when Roosevelt and Churchill, Vichy and Giraud, the awakening parties of the Third Republic and the communist-dominated sector of the Resistance had a different concept of France's future, Bernanos threw his passionate nature into the combat. From his morally elevated position, Bernanos did not judge like the self-righteous and certainly not like an avenged Cassandra, personally satisfied that his predictions have come true; he judged like suffering France herself; that is he tried to mitigate the evil he condemned and to give solace wherever it was needed. Bernanos once wrote of Maurras that the latter did not really care what happened in the public sphere, provided history confirmed his prophecies; his own war-time writings never refer to *Les Grands Cimetières sous la lune* as if saying, "I told you so!"

But this book, torn from the depths of his indignation, actually served as a perfect system of reference for the France of Vichy. I have said that what particularly filled Bernanos with alarm during the Spanish Civil War was his knowledge that Frenchmen were waiting to play the same roles the Spaniards had assumed. France also had its Popular Front and officers' clique, its "clerical" and "intellectual" parties, its Franco, its pro-Germans and admirers of Mussolini. As Bernanos had denounced Franco, he now denounced Pétain who "had stepped out of French history on the day of the surrender and will never re-enter it." For him the whole Vichy regime was "nothing but a crack, a gap, a hiatus, a vacuum on the surface of France."[21] And he acknowledged no extenuating circumstances for anyone of those who were not inalterably opposed to Pétain; he could not conceive of bargaining with the nation's honor, and put in the same category the out-and-out collaborators, the temporizers, the lukewarm and the anti-Fascist conservatives. There was no difference in his eyes among Laval, the real power behind Pétain; Darnand, the organizer of the sinister militia; Admiral Laborde, who scuttled the French fleet at Toulon; or Giraud, who escaped from a German fortress, but opposed de Gaulle and retained the substance of conservative, right-wing mentality.

"People sometimes ask me," Bernanos wrote, "what I think of General Giraud. *Mon Dieu*, it is quite simple. Like Pétain, Giraud is held responsible for the protection of a certain degenerate French bourgeoisie which has lost its national sense through avarice and fear, and which had hoped in 1940 to obtain from Hitler a guarantee for its safes, at the price of sacrificing the country."[22]

For Bernanos the category of collaborators included not only certain persons close either to Vichy or its spirit, but the French bourgeoisie as such, its mode of thinking and way of life. This did not prevent him from distinguishing the various motivations which led to collaboration and the forms collaboration assumed. He correctly diagnosed those elements in the French tradition and way of life—individualism, distrust of the modern world, love of the soil—which are to the Frenchmen's credit, but which, under the circumstances, played into the hands of Hitler, who knew how to exploit them. Naturally, some collaborators believed in Hitler the way many Germans believed in him (or for that matter, many Englishmen and Americans). He was to be a bulwark against communism or a man who would "clean up the mess"—teach the workers respect for their employers and discipline the intellectuals. But precisely because many people were convinced in a vague way that Hitler would bring "order," "discipline" or a "restoration of tradition," they fashioned their own collaboration—its sincerity, extent and translation into action—according to these personal ideas.

What seemed scandalous to Bernanos was that collaboration with the enemy became an almost normal expression of nationalism; those who before the war excluded entire classes of people from the category of "real Frenchmen," who were habitually speaking in the name of the "real France," were obviously happy and felt avenged by German presence on French soil. Whether humiliated by this presence or not, they seemed willing to endure the Germans on condition that their domestic political enemies suffered too. Thus the civil war Bernanos had predicted for France actually took place under German eyes, and the Right was protected by German arms in an even more humiliating manner than the Franquist forces had been in Spain.

GERMANY'S LUNA PARK

One of the most dangerous forms that intellectual collaboration assumed was the acceptance of a new role for France in Hitler's new Europe. France was to be an agricultural hinterland for German industrial monopoly over the continent. The collaborationists could plausibly argue that France had never been more than half-heartedly industrialized, that the "genius" of the French people was opposed to the way of life, ugliness, monotony and unthinking discipline that machine-civilization requires. In a sense, they were right. French industry traditionally rejected the techniques and methods of mass-production and emphasized uniqueness, artistic sense and quality over quantity. Even French socialism, as I have pointed out, had incorporated from its early nineteenth century beginnings, the spirit and the attitudes of the guild and was more a social-political-ideological movement than an industrial organization. French socialist leaders had opposed Marx's ideas for France because they saw that they would lead to the creation of a proletariat as miserable as that of England.

This anti-Marxist, individualist tendency of French labor survived into the twentieth century, and the Vichy regime would have tried to encourage it even without German presence. But it was catastrophic to do so when it could only benefit the Germans; and it was irresponsible of writers, publicists and intellectuals to sing the praises of the peaceful, idyllic life Frenchmen could live in the shadow of the Reich as "Germany's vegetable garden and Luna Park," to quote the pro-Nazi Marcel Déat. The eulogy of pastoral, agricultural life was, of course, not mainly German-inspired; it was, rather, the reaction of the twentieth-century intellectual against the totalitarian techniques and thought-abolishing uniformity of machine-civilization. A Jacques Chardonne, for example, argued that a state-directed economy could not maintain itself without "the disappearance of liberty, without a horrible bureaucracy, an ever-present police, the death of thinking and of art, hatred for the Christian religion and for the sense of criticism—finally without a permanent mobilization of the population."[23]

Now, there are few people who, in the course of the last fifty years have denounced technical civilization more vehemently than Bernanos himself. In fact, as we shall see, he did not even consider it a civilization, that is a phase in the historical continuity of mankind, but rather a break with everything human; not *history*, but its *liquidation*. But his patriotic sense prevailed, and he repeatedly warned his compatriots not to listen to the voices which were vaunting the charms of an agricultural paradise. In fact, he reminded his readers and listeners that this "back to the land" slogan was the more dangerous as it was embedded in the French tradition and found a naturally favorable echo in their hearts. The difference was serious, and Bernanos knew it: the instinct was now erected into a policy, officially encouraged. While the cream of skilled workers was drafted for work in German factories, at home Frenchmen were told to return to the fields. "The Germans," Bernanos warned, "preach the return of Frenchmen to the land, secretly encouraging the *aurea mediocritas* of agricultural nations . . . They make you believe that if you leave the tool for the plough, you will thereby protect France as a peaceful nation. Why not become herbivorous, imbeciles? Do you think you would then excite any the less the appetites of the carnivores? On the contrary, they would find you even more appetizing!"[24]

If French conservatism blocked anything but marginal changes, it encouraged, by its origin, its motivation and its philosophy, the development of anti-democratic feelings and policies. This was no longer a trend but a reality, actively pursued by the collaborators through laws, decrees and structural changes in the body politic, through new government organs and institutions, as well as through the press, the radio and official pronouncements.

It is hard to tell what role German-Nazi principles played in what was also a part of the genuinely French anti-democratic tradition of Maurras. But again, as in the case with the back-to-the-land movement, the flowering of anti-democratic attitudes was only possible because of German presence and this in turn deprived it of any moral basis and intellectual honesty. In the light of the Nazi occupation, the Maurrassian teachings only served to justify the invaders and the collaborators in that, ironically, the doctrine was utilized for the demoralization of the population and the discreditation of true French nationalism. "The collaborators," notes Henri Massis, perhaps the closest disciple of Maurras, "write big books filled with what they call our disintegration. . . . When a man is stepping with delight on his beaten homeland as on a corpse, he is easily persuaded that he actually tries to shake life into it. This is how some Frenchmen have slipped, almost without noticing it, from a critique of democracy into anti-democratic passion, and from there into an anti-national passion."[25]

Part of the tragedy of Vichy—a tragedy on so many counts —consisted in trying to reform the country and build a new state in a very short time, under the eyes of the occupying power. Thus whether the reforms were sincerely conceived or not, whether they were beneficial or harmful, they were most often stamped with the repulsive term of collaboration. Or the fact that certain laws were not decreed by a French government free within its borders, but by a necessarily collaborationist government under German pressure and with Nazi ideological approval was overlooked. When, for example, the first anti-Jewish laws of Justice Minister Raphael Alibert were promulgated in 1941, they were defended by reference to Church doctrine and Church practice (until 1789). Alibert and Xavier Vallat's Commissariat for Jewish Affairs even went so far as to inquire, through Léon Bérard, Vichy's ambassador to the Vatican, what high-ranking Church officials thought of the laws and their conformity with Catholic teaching.[26]

MAURRAS' NATIONALISM

Insofar as most of Pétain's and Laval's policy-making personnel were drawn from Maurrassian circles, the principles of the National Revolution and of Pétain's dictatorship must be, in the last analysis, imputed to Maurras. In the last tragic years of this representative of French nationalism, Bernanos' presentiments were borne out by events. *Scandale de la vérité,* which Bernanos wrote during the war, is a long, dolorous accusation of Maurras and the inexorable logic of his doctrine. After denouncing the "facility with which Maurras rallied to the dictators," Bernanos once more looked for the causes of this attitude in the conflicts of Maurras' inner life. He saw in Maurras a man divided against himself, passionately admiring the *discipline* of a certain line of thought while refusing its *content.* I think that the sense of the Bernanosian diagnosis is that he finally came to consider Maurras a *romantic* repelled by his own inclination and reacting against it by developing a purely intellectual admiration for the *classical,* that is for the severe, the pure line. Bernanos called this inner cleavage "one of the cruellest forms of damnation in this world," and saw in the France of Vichy the incarnation of Maurras' infernal soul: "The France of Maurras is as hollow, as vacuous as his Catholicism deprived of Christ, as his concept of Catholic order deprived of grace."[27]

Maurras is held responsible for the cadre of Vichy, for the high and low level collaborators. Those formed by him are "dried up intellectuals," "beasts with opinions" (*bêtes à jugement*), who have Maurras' "carnal hatred" for other peoples' thoughts. Without a trace of charity and generosity, these disciples of Maurras have confiscated the State and the Church, and have isolated them from the world of the people, from the workers. They are like Thiers' conservatives who repressed the Commune; ever since, "the current of Maurras' ideas has followed its course through the deep layers of the conservative bourgeoisie and finally took a turn towards dictatorship."[28]

Thus Bernanos came to judge nationalism by its Maurrassian-Pétainist fruit: "The respect I feel for the memory of Maurice Barrès," he admitted now, "cannot prevent me from saying that nationalism was invented to solve certain cases of conscience which are more literary than political, and to provide a man-made faith, a man-made religion for men of letters who are de-Christianized to the root of their souls."[29] De-Christianized and, as we have seen, de-nationalized at the same time; for Bernanos, this was almost the same thing, and the figure and fate of Saint Joan of Arc were the key to both. Just as he had compared on many occasions the beginning of the fifteenth with the beginning of the twentieth century, and given their respective contemporary roles to the English occupants, the treacherous Burgundians, the pompous French prelates in foreign pay, the timid Dauphin and to Joan herself, he now scorned again the "realists" who were betting on German victory as their fifteenth-century ancestors had been betting on English victory. "Your Vichy-masters," he told his audience through the Brazzaville radio, "did not believe yesterday in the victory of France. Even to desire it, is impossible for them today; they can only fear it. If a new miracle of God—as in former ages—liberated our cities, opened for us the road to

Rheims, they would vow their forces against Joan of Arc as their predecessors did in the fifteenth century . . . German victory alone could save their skin."[30]

As at the time of the Spanish Civil War, Bernanos was watching closely the attitude of the French clergy. In spite of his Majorcan impressions, he expected the hierarchy and Catholics in general to understand what was at stake and to become the vanguard of resistance. The contact with popular forces and with workingmen, which had been lost for the Church in the social battles of the nineteenth and twentieth centuries, could have been regained now when all Frenchmen, workers and priests, soldiers, and civil servants, discovered a bond of unity in their love for their threatened country. Bernanos' warnings, therefore, were addressed on a tone of a particular urgency to his fellow Catholics, pointing out to them the fallacies of the collaborationist policy and the dangers of welcoming such laws of Vichy which seemed to be inspired by a religious spirit.

"French Catholics," he said to them, "the entire nation knows that it is in the hands of an unpopular minority which, for twenty years, has sought in vain a chance to rule and which has only found it in the disaster of our country."[31] In other words, Bernanos knew that Vichy was to be an interlude only; therefore, in proportion as French Catholics identified themselves with it, as they were favored by its laws, as the hierarchy turned sympathetically towards the regime, the ruder would be the awakening and the greater the loss for the French Church in the long run. Like many others, Bernanos dreaded the day when Vichy would declare war upon the British and the Americans and send its troops into battle blessed by its prelates. This is perhaps the reason why, in a token yet moving gesture, he addressed his most significant war-time writing to the Anglo-Saxon nations (*Lettre aux Anglais* which includes a *Letter aux Américains*) as if to apologize in advance for what his misled countrymen might do against them.

Bernanos knew with what feeling of comfort his countrymen

were ready to settle down under the inglorious shadow of Vichy, because he had measured their selfishness and short-sightedness after Munich. His voice rang with anguish lest humiliation become for them a way of life, duplicity an accepted technique of the State and the execution of German-dictated measures an easy shelter for their consciences. He warned the clergy to be a watchful guardian and guide of these consciences: "If the collectivity, the Leader, the State or the Party are recognized, by the Church, as capable of assuming responsibility for the most atrocious actions, the average Catholic who has committed them has a perfect right to receive Holy Communion afterwards. How can you then expect this Christian not to form, in the long run, the same idea of the omnipotent State as does a disciple of Hitler"?[32]

Bernanos correctly evaluated the poison distilled in the minds of Frenchmen by Nazi propaganda which, clumsy as it was, nevertheless did sometimes attack in subtle ways: "Nazi propaganda has not weakened the religious, moral or patriotic sentiment, it has disfigured it under the pretense of paying it homage. It has implanted in people's consciences a false religion, a false morality, a false patriotism, a false heroism, a false sense of honor."[33]

It was imperative that Frenchmen understand Hitler's diabolical strategy, which aimed at the moral disintegration of France followed by its complete political domination and eventual incorporation into the Germanic world; collaboration was not only unpatriotic and immoral, it was also useless: even if Germany won the war, it would reject the collaborators who served German purposes only by being "ferments of decomposition dissolving the moral fibre of France." As far as French Catholics were concerned, since they were especially wooed by Vichy and behind Vichy by German occupation policy, they should be even more wary of collaboration: "There is not one Catholic in the world stupid enough to believe that once a German peace is secured, Hitler will agree to become the well-intentioned speculator of a Christian renaissance. He knows very well that such a renaissance would sooner or later be directed against him, against totalitarian nationalism and racism."[34]

With these relentless attacks on collaborationist policy, Bernanos hoped to weaken the seductive argument that the Germans would grant France an important role in post-war Europe. It must be understood that Vichy policy was based on the assumption that Germany was defending the continent against Soviet Russia and against Bolshevization and that this tremendous effort required the war-time occupation of all Europe. The harshness of the occupation, the racial laws, deportations, forced draft of workers and attempt to build up in France a one-party system could be explained by the partisans of Vichy as German emergency measures which would be cancelled after Russia's defeat. The most prominent advocate of collaboration, Pierre Laval himself, told Mr. Ralph Heinzen, United Press Representative in the un-occupied zone and his longtime confidant, that Hitler had agreed that "after the war was over, France would play a big role in the new Europe." Laval interpreted the agreement with Hitler "as a guarantee of French independence in the post-war Europe as well as a guarantee of the integrity of continental France and of the French Empire."[35] Yet, it is quite likely that not even Laval himself was fully convinced of Hitler's good intentions: indeed, to others he apparently confessed strong distrust of the Reich and also his determination "to defend the interests of France and the French people against a victorious Germany by all possible means."[36]

Whatever Laval's personal hopes and fears were, the general climate spread by collaboration was that of the obligation to do a kind of penance for their pre-war way of life, alleged frivolity, errors of judgment; collaborationist speakers and penpushers outbade each other in denouncing everything that had happened under the Third Republic from pro-British orientation to Gide's influence on youth. With the subtle encouragement of German propaganda experts, they pointed out the undisciplined character of Frenchmen, their incurable preference for good cheer and equally incurable distaste for constructive virtues and collective enterprises, the conditions of national greatness.

As Vichy pushed Frenchmen of both zones towards humility and obedience to the Germans, inviting them to beat their breasts and repeat a collective *mea culpa*, the farce became intolerable. Jean-Paul Sartre describes the atmosphere which prevailed at the time in Paris in these lines: "In moments when we were almost ready to yield to remorse, the people of Vichy and their collaborators held us back by trying to push us further into that mood. The occupation was not only the constant presence of the victors in our towns; it was also, on the walls and in the papers, the repulsive image in which we were expected to find our own features. The collaborators began by appealing to our good faith. We are beaten, they said, let us be fair players; let us recognize our faults. And immediately they added: 'Let us admit that the Frenchman is light-minded, a braggart and an egotist; that he does not understand the first thing about other nations, that the war took our country by surprise, and in a state of disintegration.' Humoristic posters were ridiculing our last hopes. Faced with so much baseness and clumsy ruse, we hardened ourselves in a desire to reconquer our pride."[37]

From far-away Brazil, Bernanos felt the humiliation of his countrymen: "We are a baptized nation," he cried out in indignation, "held to the Gospels, not to the Old Testament; we cannot be treated like rebellious Jews delivered by Jahweh into the hands of the Babylonians or the Ninivites. When a father punishes us, he should not expect us to roll in the dust like beasts."[38] Not that Vichy had the right to play the avenging father; Bernanos considered the regime, as we have seen, a shameful interregnum in an otherwise glorious history, so shameful in fact that "not even victory itself could efface the

spot of having handed over the refugee Jews to the Germans
and the refugee Spanish republicans to Franco."[39]

In a particularly violent passage, Bernanos demanded that
ex-Minister Georges Mandel, held prisoner and about to be
delivered to the Gestapo be left unharmed and released: "If
your masters do not give us back Mandel alive, you will have to
pay such a high price for this Jewish blood that it will astound
the world. Every drop of that Jewish blood is more precious to
us than all the purple of a fascist cardinal's cloak—you better
take note of this, Admirals, Marshals, Excellencies, Eminences
and Reverend Fathers!"[40]

THE RESISTANCE

The war-time writings of Bernanos establish unequivocally
the fact that he was moving closer to a "resistant's position, in
the general sense of denouncing the Vichy government and
analyzing the forces which composed it, of accepting de
Gaulle's leadership and his principles of liberation and of con-
tributing the influence of his voice and pen to the French war
effort. He mentioned repeatedly and proudly that two of his
sons and a beloved nephew were fighting in the Gaullist forces;
he eagerly accepted the invitation of Gaullist broadcasters to
address his countrymen on various occasions; and, last not least,
he became a focus of the French spirit—and of French letters—
in South America. Without giving up one of his convictions,
Bernanos was "resisting" in the company of men whom fifteen
years earlier he would probably have attacked on many issues.

Why did Bernanos commit himself so uncompromisingly to
the Resistance? What did he expect of it for his country? First
of all, his profound instinct for French history told him that
what France needed most was a moral regeneration, not artificial and imposed like the one preached by the "Tartufes of
Vichy," but one which is born in the fire of exaltation and
sacrifice. That the Resistance was the moral heir of Joan of Arc

was, for him, almost a supernatural truth. Consequently, "before the enemy, the Resistance is France once more on her feet. Freed from the enemy, it must become France on the march."[41] In this way, the Resistance movement was the miraculous link, bridging the gap represented by Vichy, and tying together, at the same time, past and future, tradition and revolution: "We must take the revolution out of the hands of a cynical and bitter world which had never understood its meaning . . . I say 'our revolution' with a calm assurance. Saying it, I feel I am in harmony with what I have always tried to serve: the cause of tradition and spirit, the soul of our people."[42]

A strange association of words—revolution, tradition, past and future—particularly at a time when, with victory near, the French Resistance was pulling in every direction. But this was no time to acknowledge the sectional struggles among communists, the home army, the socialists, the M.R.P., the Algerian Gaullists, and so on. The movement still converged in de Gaulle's hands and presented a unified front to the outsider. In Bernanos' conception, the men of the Resistance, in spite of their divergent inspirations, were those "free men" who had a high idea of service to the country and who were "in the straight line of France's history." He had never been a democrat, nor did he claim a change of heart now; he could only laugh at the naive assumption that the "country's future will depend on universal suffrage." It would take much more to reconcile Frenchmen and establish order. In fact, he told General de Gaulle himself shortly after he returned from Brazil, that the mediocrities in his entourage and his government would soon overwhelm his most noble plans, as they always manage to do with everything exceptional. The fact, however, that so many people wanted to climb on the Gaullist bandwagon did not surprise him. He thought that this was the price to pay for the absence of a true French victory, because, after all, victory was due to the liberating armies under foreign command.

In other words, Bernanos was not starry-eyed about the

Resistance; yet he believed, in the last two years of the war, that it would become the nucleus of rebirth, having passed the test of patriotism, and having pledged martyrs in such a number that their accumulated moral capital would serve as a foundation for a new France. Bernanos did not believe that Joan of Arc's life and works had made of the France of Charles VII and of Louis XI an exemplary land of virtue and happiness; nor did he believe in the moral perfection of post-war Frenchmen. But he had always conceived of a nation or a society as of the Church, that is, as a mystical communion in which the martyrs and true leaders lend their intense faith and the fruits of their sacrifice to the whole collective body, enabling the latter to benefit by these free gifts in innumerable ways. "I have always believed, and I believe now more than ever, that the existence of a nation, as the existence of an individual, is linked to the presence in its vital sphere of certain very precious elements. Their gradual disappearance may, at first, go unnoticed, until the day when the proportion drops under the minimum threshold and the patient collapses, as if struck by lightning."[43]

These few words summarize Bernanos' hopes for and disappointments with the Resistance. He had at first insisted on believing that the men grouped in the Resistance were the "precious elements" that would revive the country, the "handful of ferment" as he wrote elsewhere, "which would raise the dough."[44] But he was forced to conclude that the heroes of the Resistance formed too strong a dose for a country in which precisely these vital elements were lacking. The French nation no longer takes to heroism, it is no longer affected by it.

This is how André Rousseaux describes his conversation with Bernanos at their first post-war meeting (in London in 1945). "We spent the day together . . . He kept asking me questions about France whose face he was to see again in a few days. He was looking forward to this encounter with infinite tenderness and immense anxiety. I told him of all the painful surprise and embarrassment we had had during the past nine months.* My narrative was rather unprecise, and it contradicted the statements I had made an hour before in public, at the lecture, concerning a better future. We did not even notice this contradiction. It was understood by both of us that this rebirth of France was burning our souls like a flame that nothing ought to extinguish . . . I still see Bernanos with my mind's eye, across from me at the table of the restaurant near Buckingham Palace where we dined that evening. 'I expected this,' he murmured, 'I expected this.' He pronounced these words in a low voice, as if under the weight of a terrible weariness. The great anger which was to burst forth a few weeks later and which was to thunder till his death, had not yet shown itself."[45]

Readers and commentators will always ask themselves whether Bernanos was a leftist or a rightist. I shall try to present the elements of this controversy in the next chapter. At present, we may formulate the issue by asking whom he blamed for the failure of this potential elite.

In 1946, Bernanos wrote: "During the war, the Resistance had been proscribed; afterwards it was cynically exploited . . . The dead who are constantly mentioned might soon play the purely honorary role that the dead of Verdun used to play in Marshal Pétain's speeches."[46]

Exploited by whom? Rousseaux mentions in his last reminiscences of Bernanos that the latter had understood, after his return to France, that the communists, capitalizing on their wartime prestige as the spear-head of the Resistance, were preparing a revolution of their own. This revolution and this elite were not, of course, what Bernanos meant when he spoke about "our revolution" and the "new incarnation of Christian honor." He did not, as a matter of fact, particularly oppose a revolution that the communists would incite; but he rejected the deadening orthodoxy and robot mentality they would bring with them.

* That is, since the Liberation, August–September, 1944.

André Rousseaux concluded that, confronted with what the Left had made of the Revolution, Bernanos became (or became again) a man of the Right. But the truth is, perhaps, less simple. Bernanos wrote later that he was not afraid of communism, only of the tyrannical state that was its outcome. This was, however, according to him the line of evolution of the democratic-capitalistic state also; his many post-war analyses of the future of France, the world, civilization, all point to a monstrous state whose heavy limbs will crush the individual, his private life, his freedom and his conscience. Thus when he denounced the events in France, he did not single out the communists, but passed judgment upon the general indifference of the nation and its elite and upon the triumph of the old routine.

The cynical exploiters of the Resistance, of that brief moment of pride and hope, were not, then, the Left or the Right, but Frenchmen in general, the mediocre counsellors of de Gaulle, the routine-loving politicians, the conservative spirit which demanded nothing more than to forget the past and continue with untroubled conscience. The imposture of the Resistance was the imposture of the abbé Cénabre who remained a priest after he had been emptied of the last trace of his vocation: the Resistance turned into a bureaucracy, living off its prestige and preparing an unheroic tomorrow.

NOTES

1. *Plea for Liberty*, p. 102.
2. *Ibid.*, p. 190.
3. *Les Grands Cimetières sous la lune*, p. 317.
4. *Ibid.*, pp. 56–7. This, of course, did not mean that the bourgeoisie would be grateful to the "new inquisitors" protecting it: "The Right never knew how to protect its friends or its accomplices . . . The spirit which animates the Right, despite

its boasting declarations, is always a spirit of concessions. It will easily concede the heads of those who will have safeguarded its interests." (*Le Chemin de la Croix-des-Ames*, I, p. 133.)

5. Charles de Gaulle, *Mémoires de Guerre* (Plon, 1954), Vol. I, *Appel* p. 26.

6. *Journal de France*, Vol. I.

7. Robert Aron, *Histoire de Vichy* (Arthème Fayard, 1954), p. 109.

8. *La France contre les Robots*, p. 111.

9. *Le Chemin de la Croix-des-Ames*, II, p. 10.—In his "Autobiographie" he writes that he opposed the armistice with Germany because this country "seemed a much greater threat to freedom than the Soviet Union, a socialist Great Britain, or an isolationist United States.

10. *La Liberté pour quoi faire?*, p. 224.

11. Interview given to the Brazilian paper, *A Noite*, October 1938.

12. *Bulletin*, Nos. 24–25, June 1955.

13. Interview in *Combat*, March 20, 1948.

14. *Les Grands Cimetières sous la lune*, pp. 358–359.

15. *War Memoirs of Charles de Gaulle* (New York: Simon and Schuster, 1959), Vol. II, *Unity*, p. 57.

16. From a speech at Rio de Janeiro, in September 1943.

17. "Croire en ce monde ou croire en nous," article in *Carrefour*, December 25, 1946. (Quoted in *Bulletin*, No. 32, August 1958.)

18. "Il fout refaire des hommes libres," article in *La Bataille*, July 26, 1948.—Compare with de Gaulle (*Unity*, pp. 77, 344): "The Third Republic was the regime which for so many, many years had floated upon the nation's surface without directing its vital forces . . . The notorious misfortunes that had rained down upon France . . . were the consequences of a long disease of the State." As de Gaulle entered Paris on August 25, 1944, his first visit was to the Ministry of War that he had left four years before and where he now wanted to set up his offices. Everything was as he had seen it last: "Not a piece of furniture, not a rug, not a curtain had been disturbed. On the desk, the telephone was in the same place, and on the call buttons exactly the same names . . . Nothing was missing

except the State. It was my duty to restore it . . . I installed my staff at once and got down to work."

19. *La France contre les Robots*, p. 36.
20. "La Dictature de la médiocrité," article in *La Bataille*, November 30, 1944.
21. *Le Chemin de la Croix-des-Ames*, I, p. 90; IV, p. 98.
22. *Ibid.*, III, p. 143.
23. Quoted by Raymond Aron in *L'Homme contre les tyrans*, (New York: Ed. de la Maison Française, 1944), p. 177.
24. *Appel aux Français*, quoted in *Bulletin*, Nos. 24–25, Juin 1955.
25. *Maurras et son temps*, II, p. 168.
26. *France during the German Occupation* (A collection of 292 statements on the government of Maréchal Pétain and Pierre Laval), Hoover Institute Documentary Series, II, pp. 626ff.
27. *Scandale de la vérité*, pp. 28, 17.
28. *Ibid.*, p. 44.
29. *Ibid.*, p. 49.
30. *Appel aux Français*, quoted in *Bulletin*, Nos. 24–25, June 1955.
31. *Le Chemin de la Croix-des-Ames*, I, p. 139.
32. *La France contre les Robots*, pp. 164–5.
33. *Le Chemin de la Croix-des-Ames*, III, p. 40.
34. *Appel aux Catholiques français*, on the B.B.C., December 1940.
35. *France during the German Occupation*, *loc. cit.*, III, p. 1601.
36. *Ibid.*, III, p. 1429,
37. "Paris sous l'occupation," in *Situations*, Vol. III.
38. *Le Chemin de la Croix-des-Ames*, IV, p. 72.
39. "Réflexions sur le cas de conscience français."
40. *Le Chemin de la Croix-des-Ames*, III, p. 316.
41. "La Dictature de la médiocrité," in *La Bataille*, November 30, 1944.
42. *La France contre les Robots*, p. 35.
43. Quoted by André Rousseaux, "La Démission de la France," in *Cahiers du Rhône* (*Essais et Témoinages*).
44. "Croire en ce monde ou croire en nous," in *Carrefour*, December 25, 1946.
45. "La Démission de la France," *loc. cit.*, p. 321.
46. *Carrefour*, December 25, 1946.

6 "My Country is the Conscience of Europe"

THE France to which Bernanos returned in the summer of 1945 was, in many respects, the same France he had left seven years before. The power relationship between various social classes, political parties and intellectual influences may have changed, and the extreme right was reduced to silence and political impotence. Yet, the old forces were to regroup surprisingly fast, and the Fourth Republic became an almost exact copy of the Third. Although de Gaulle, in his war-time proclamations, had announced a "social and economic revolution," it was, after all, up to the traditional parties to interpret its meaning according to their own ideological commitments, parliamentary routine and future prospects.

On the Left, where the communists were now in a privileged position, the revolution meant, first, a spectacular purge of all collaborators, real or so branded, and second, the proclamation of a new regime, pleasing Moscow, perhaps a "people's democracy." Léon Blum's party, on the other hand, remained loyal to the democratic-parliamentary structure, but within this framework the clandestine, war-time leadership of the socialists demanded the socialization of the country's economy and had even fixed a dead-line: after two years of emergency government by de Gaulle.

The Catholic center had detected the ultimate goals of the

communist plan, but, not unreasonably, the leaders of its party,
the *Mouvement Républicain Populaire*, were hoping that their
presence in any conceivable coalition would counter-balance
communist strategy. They thought that the reintegration of
large numbers of Catholic votes loyal to the Republic would
be a guarantee of equilibrium. But in spite of the prestige of a
Georges Bidault, over-all head of the Resistance, and of
François Mauriac, enthusiastic for the prospects of a Christian
socialism, the Catholics were not united.

There remained, in the first place, those who, compromised
or not by Vichy, still clung to the pre-war ideals of the traditional Right; for them de Gaulle's *Rassemblement du Peuple
Français* was to be an unexpected haven, just as the Gaullist
U.N.R. was to be after May 13, 1958. In the meantime, considering themselves victimized by the purge, they reproached
the regime for filling the important posts in the administration,
police and army with members of the Resistance. Then there
were others who, playing no political role but possessing intellectual prestige, concerned themselves less with one or another
class of the population, the workers or the bourgeois, than with
the cultural and spiritual survival of the nation as a whole. In
their eyes Hitler, the fascist decades and Vichy were the manifestations of the eternal evil against which modern times and societies are not better protected than any preceding age and
nation. They, of course, admitted the necessity of solicitude
for the welfare of the proletariat; they even considered that in
the face of communist propaganda, reinforced by the prestige
of war-time sacrifice, a clear reaffirmation of the Catholic
principles of social justice was indeed an urgent task. But they
were unwilling to see the proletariat in a romantic light suffused
with religion and the worker as Christ crucified.

Finally, there were the *Catholiques de gauche* or Catholic
progressives, willing to take a sympathetic view, if not of communist ideology, at least of the social protest which the communists voiced. But even the ideological part was easy to swallow

if doses of Hegelianism could be added to the strong Marxian purgative. The Hegelian system was indeed granted by leftist Catholic intellectuals the honor of a revelation, as important in the political order as the Christian revelation is in the spiritual order. Thus it became acceptable to speak of an atheistic phase in history if this were necessary for the ultimate shaping of a better world. For their neglect of the proletariat, the bourgeoisie and the Church associated with it were to pay the penalty of standing aside while the working class developed its independent consciousness. In this period, as Jean Lacroix has put it, "Marxism remains the imminent philosophy of the proletariat."

Thus, after 1945, both Left and Right, Catholics and progressives, started out burdened with memories, but also light with the immense hope that came to them from all quarters of the population. In the general jubilation created by the departure of the Germans, the excesses of the improvised tribunals and the uncontrollable acts of vengeance of individuals and gangs did not pass unnoticed; but they were ascribed, at least by those who were not the victims, to the justified wrath of an oppressed and persecuted nation. As these acts were, in a way, considered the prelude of a revolution, the majority of the people did not stop to deplore them; those who did, were decried as enemies of the coming better world. Anyway, passions soon quieted down, the new Constitution was voted in,* and the political life of the Fourth Republic, its gravitational center slightly shifted towards the Left, took up where the Third had left it. Frenchmen could say once more: *plus ça change, plus c'est la même chose.*

In a different sense, Bernanos had not changed either during the years spent abroad. As he had not rejoiced after the first World War, so he was less than optimistic now.

---

* Approving the Constitution were 9,000,000 votes; against 7,800,000; another 7,880,000 abstained.

The classifiers still found it impossible to "situate" him, and, as always in such cases, they decided that he was much too vague: eloquent, but not really relevant. "Since I have returned from America," Bernanos told an audience, "people say that I am often right, but they reproach me for not drawing any conclusions. What do they mean by concluding? Do they mean adopting a system? Joining a party?"[1] But systems, in his judgment, were pompous vacuities, collections of slogans on which the "masses" could be induced to fall asleep. Already in a Brazilian notebook he had remarked that the "role of the honest man, the aristocrat of the spirit, is to encourage a state of freedom among his contemporaries, a state of mind which rebels against systems." And he added, "Systems invade only decaying civilizations."[2]

In spite of the "vagueness," "untimeliness," and "traditionalism" he is reproached with, Bernanos' prestige is universally high even among those who do not share his religious faith or political convictions. How is one to explain this fact?

Primarily, the reader has the definite impression that the novels he admires and the political writings which force his response are of the same inspiration; he feels that the writer stands behind every word, that no consideration of politics, personal ambition or need for systematization is wedged between the writer and himself. Secondly, the reader understands that what he loses through lack of a system, he gains through the writer's total and passionate commitment to the great problems of contemporary man; he finds himself in the presence not only of a thinking man, but also a feeling man who communicates to him his visceral reactions to the modern world. As Emmanuel Mounier wrote of him: "There is terror in Bernanos' vision of contemporary man, a physical terror, a terror of the flesh."[3] Thirdly, what makes Bernanos unique among critics of contemporary man and society—and so different from, let us say, Ortega y Gasset and his elegant, erudite demonstrations—is that he made no secret of the fact that he saw the present spiritual crisis in terms of France's own inner dilemma and that he judged the world's future with reference to the place France was going to occupy in it. Thus in the last years of his life, Bernanos became increasingly preoccupied with the study of three problems, related to one another like concentric circles. The questions he raised in his books, pamphlets, and lectures of this most mature period, may be grouped under these headings: How to save France from the madness of the modern world? How to save the world from the excesses of mechanized civilization? How to save the individual from the pressure of the collectivity and from an increasingly powerful State?

These problems were not of course separated in Bernanos' own powerful and prophetic vision. Although I shall speak of the first in the present chapter, and discuss the other two in the next, they ought, in the final view, to be seen as a whole.

THE STATE VS. FRANCE

Charles Maurras wrote that there is no absolute assurance that France will survive for ever. There is a need for constant effort—this is the essence of civilization—to maintain a thing so fragile as a community of men. Bernanos' notion of France was, perhaps, less exclusive and intolerant than that of Maurras, but more spiritual and more truly mystical. In a sense, all his works, including his novels, deal with France; with the exception of Les Grands Cimetières, they describe French events, take place on French soil and search out French problems. In another sense, however, they deal with the eternally human as reflected in France, in the French soul and history. His confidence in the destiny of France is Christian in inspiration, whereas the basic pessimism of Maurras strikes a late pagan tone, that of the dying Roman Empire. Bernanos refused to surrender to the monstrous forces he denounced because he stubbornly believed that Divine Providence rules the universe and that France, the finest fruit of man's achievement, has a supernatural backing. Thus his country was for him at once the guarantee of the ultimate survival of freedom in the world, *and* the sensitive instrument which measures mankind's state of spiritual integrity. "My country," he wrote, "is the heart and the conscience of Europe; this does not mean that it is more precious than the others, but that it reacts more vividly to good as well as to evil. It is the first to get the disease and the first to be cured."

The message Bernanos was carrying in his last years to various corners of the French-speaking West—Geneva, Brussels, North Africa—was, first of all, a message of France as he conceived it. The most urgent task was, in his judgment, to reassure those who look to France for guidance, that it had not succumbed to any of the modern diseases: ideology, machine civilization, the tyranny of the State, depersonalization, indifference to freedom. He had learned in Brazil that for many people all over the world France was still the home of the individual and his finest values, and he thought that if the South American jungle-dweller listens with anxiety to his radio for news about France's war against Germany, the neighbors of his country will be so much more eager to hear about its role in the new, even more pervasive war against universal barbarization.

For this is what Bernanos now foresaw with a frightening lucidity: the all encompassing reign of the *machines* and of the *multitudes* in comparison to which the struggle against the overt dictatorships had been an honorable duel with clean weapons. "If you do not watch out," he wrote in *Lettre aux Anglais*, "what the dictators wanted to achieve in a few years will materialize in fifty or a hundred; the result will be the same: the State will have conquered all, gained all, absorbed all; you will have escaped the totalitarian demi-gods only to let yourselves slip slowly into the glue of an anonymous dictatorship."[4] The rock in the mounting morass, Bernanos asserted, was France: "France is still a *patrie*; that is quite a different thing than the political and economic organization which tends to be confused with the modern State . . . [This new State] is half usurer, half policeman, with eyes on the keyhole and hands in the citizens' pockets. [France is still a *patrie*] that is a moral being . . . who does not claim a right to everything in the name of the same law which applies to animals, sacrifices the bee to the hive and the individual to the species."[5]

It is important to penetrate the fundamental thinking which dictated Bernanos' view of the world and of his own time. It is evident from his novels, and I have pointed this out at various occasions in previous chapters, that he considered the world, as does every Christian writer and philosopher, as the stage of the struggle between good and evil, without, of course, identifying anybody or any category as the carrier, beyond forgiveness and redemption, of the total burden of evil. In this way, Bernanos did not believe, as Maurras did, that certain people and races are forever sick and guilty—microbes of disease, so to speak—but he had a firm and at the same time nuanced conviction about the existence and reality of evil in this world which necessitates alertness and ceaseless combat. Instead of the ridiculous optimism of the mealy-mouthed who expected everlasting peace, social justice and universal happiness after the second World War, Bernanos knew that the war would continue, against a different enemy and with different weapons. In an article, "We Are At War," he wrote: "This is the war of states against societies, of States against *patries*—of states which are stronger everyday, against societies which are weaker, against *patries* losing their flesh and bone . . . The modern state has slowly reached this phase of growth, beyond which it can only be a fantastic instrument of constraint and enslavement. The State is now a technique in action for the dispossession of real men and for the profit of the future robot."[6]

France, then, refuses to become a State in the modern sense; it is not responsible for machine civilization and instinctively

opposes it. "French civilization, heir to the civilization of
Greece, has labored for many centuries to create free men, that
is, men wholly responsible for their actions; France will not
enter the Robot Paradise."[7] Repeatedly, Bernanos pointed out
that while technology has been an ever-present threat in mankind's struggle with nature, historically the usurpation of technology began in England. He mentioned only French resistance
to mechanization in industry, the Lyons weavers' strike in the
early 1830's, for example, trying to support his point that the
French genius had been, throughout the nineteenth century,
reluctant to adopt the new ways. Thus, he states, "France is
not responsible for this absurd civilization which has been made
without her, against her. Facing this world, France is free. I
believe that France alone is capable of imagining and creating
another world, of imagining and creating it with that prodigious sensibility of the intelligence which breathes life into
ideas."[8]

All this may well be irritating, but it should be remembered
that Bernanos was not an aggressive nationalist like Maurras.
With Maurras, nationalism was an ideology, a policy, a plan of
action; with Bernanos, patriotism was a supernatural duty—
a duty to remain human and linked to God, to continue living
by bread and by faith. To be a patriot, for him, was as natural
a task as to be religious and therefore essentially *open* towards
others, not *closed* as the Maurrassian doctrine implies. Much
has been said about "the civilizing mission of France," but it
has been said by diplomats, professors, cultural organizations
and textbooks, with the result that the expression has become
a platitude; but Bernanos lived it as a reality. His vehemence
against the *bien-pensants*, Munich, the armistice, Vichy, against
the abuses of the Liberation, cannot be understood except in the
light of his horrified indignation that France was betraying itself. And his vivid hopes that his country would again resist,
and resist better, against machines and robots, were born from

the desire that by saving the world for freedom, France would redeem itself.

CHRISTIAN SOCIALISM

What were the concrete conditions of such a redemption? What were the views of Bernanos about his country's situation and immediate future? Did he lean, after his return, towards one more than another political party or towards a support of de Gaulle? Did he favor the newly formed parties in Europe which combined a democratic orientation with Christian doctrines? Having long before and resolutely abandoned Maurras, did Bernanos get nearer the Left, under the banner of the Church or otherwise? Or was André Rousseaux right when he wrote that, disillusioned with the degeneration of the Resistance, Bernanos became again a man of the Right?

It is not easy to answer these questions. Bernanos had no programs to present, no organizations to set up. The inspiration behind his social criticism and behind his philosophy of man was not of a type which could be translated into concrete terms of action. What he wished to present in his articles and lectures was a certain spirit and mentality—that of free men against robots, of a humane civilization against the liquidation of the human being by the joint and inhuman rule of collectivism and technology.

Basing one's opinion on several pre-war and war-time statements, one would have expected to see the returning Bernanos militate in the ranks of the *Mouvement Républicain Populaire*. His sympathy for the "petit peuple" at every phase of French history, for the Revolution of 1789, for socialism *à la Proudhon*, for the workers of the Commune insurrection could have oriented him towards a form of socialism which had the stamp of Church approval on it. The M.R.P. seemed to be an organization fulfilling these conditions and grouping the new elite Bernanos had expected to emerge from the Resistance.

The M.R.P. was indeed a new party in every respect, untrammeled by the routine of the pre-war parties. Its origins were respectable: during the occupation there took place a sincere encounter of hearts and minds between men with opposing convictions. For reasons that are easy to understand, this exchange of ideas contributed, in general, more to a widening of the Catholic conservative horizon than that of its adversary which felt comfortably carried by the main stream of history. Catholics learned, first of all, that if they wanted to avoid the mistakes which wrecked the pre-war Right, they must make numerous concessions to the social preoccupations of the century and adopt certain "leftist" methods of organization and propaganda. This was understood to be the price of remaining a candidate for power or at least influential not only with the middle-classes but also with the proletariat. Accordingly, the M.R.P. prepared for the elections by presenting a program as vast as possible and by taking advantage of its leaders' wartime association with General de Gaulle. It had made itself known as the "party of loyalty" to the General and promised to make good the latter's promise of "prosperity through a transformed social and economic regime." In fact, at the 1946 elections, the M.R.P. received four and a half million votes, unexpectedly large in view of the Fourth Republic's initial leftist orientation. This success seemed to authorize the leaders of the M.R.P. to pursue their goal of constituting a large Catholic and social party, occupying a stabilizing central position in the nation's political life.

Bernanos easily could have played an important political role, either in the M.R.P. or outside of it. His prestige was considerable because he embodied the qualities that the Resistance admired: courage, dedication, integrity and patriotism, and he was politically "innocent," that is, uncompromised either by Left or by Right. When de Gaulle, on the recommendation of friends, decided to offer Bernanos and his family the expenses for the transatlantic crossing, he may have wished not only to honor the great writer, but also to enlist the collaboration of a politically unstained figure, an independent man.

Witnesses have since told the story of the encounter between Bernanos and de Gaulle, the man of fiery temperament and the man of marble, who yet had the same image of France. The General-Prime Minister offered Bernanos the post of Minister of Education. Thereupon the storm broke out; in a long outburst against the mediocrity which he saw submerging France again, Bernanos indignantly refused, telling de Gaulle that he was no bureaucrat or file-clerk and that he could not imagine himself sitting behind a desk and running a machinery. The interview was brief; the General listened attentively but did not answer. Bernanos left in a high state of agitation. He was to tell lecture-audiences afterwards that there were three posts in which, given his past and personality, he could not visualize himself: that of Minister, Academician and Archbishop; the first two, he said, had been offered to him, but he refused; the third had not been offered yet. The question may be asked if he was wise to refuse a post in which he would have had a considerable influence over matters that lay so close to his heart. Or did he become aware, in the decisive moment, of the compromises he would be forced into? The burden of absolute commitment is heavy on a man's life.

What was the relationship between Bernanos and the ideal and the program of the M.R.P., or rather, between him and the concept of a Christian Socialist party? The question raises any number of essential issues: Bernanos' views on the Church and democracy, the participation of Catholics in public life, the responsibilities of government and the possibility of rapport with communists.

Bernanos always had a vivid understanding of social justice and the plight of workers. Although he favored the old forms of worker-master relationship, the guild system and the individual forms of production, he had no illusion concerning the exploitation from which the inferior classes always suffered.

He condemned the cruelty of old industrial establishments as well as the impersonality of the new: "When, after a last inventory," he wrote with sarcasm, "the old master glassmaker calculated the exact figure of his profit, he had, perhaps, a thought for his modest collaborator, who, meanwhile, was spitting up the last remnants of his lungs into the cold ashes of the fireplace, between the slumbering mangy cat and the cradle where a misbegotten child, with an old man's head, was yelling for food."[9] But he held the conviction that the economic question could neither be settled as a part of a political solution—as Maurras thought—nor as a result of humanitarian sentiments applied to the problem. In other words, both the nationalists and the democrats had a distorted image of reality, because one left out of consideration the modern conditions of the world and the other ignored the religious nature of man.

First of all, Bernanos did not believe in the possible restoration of the old forms of society, organized according to hierarchy and inspired by religious faith. A society based on the corporatist system was inconceivable now that the State was levelling and absorbing all the intermediary bodies within the nation, leaving not freedom but only equality. Furthermore, after the lessons of Vichy, there was no guarantee that the advocates of medieval social structure and religious inspiration, those who quoted Church councils and papal encyclicals, would in any way improve the conditions of society within a nationalist framework of the State. Indeed, Bernanos had warned from Brazil that the people of Europe, after the war, should not work together with those who had prepared the defeat and scoffed at freedom.

On the other hand, he equally condemned the optimists and humanitarians who put all their trust in reforms and blueprints, and who, on the Christian side, equate sentimentalism with religion. "Do you want a society without poor?" he asked them; "You will have, instead, an inhuman society. Innocent poverty which you think you will have destroyed, will reappear under other, frightening forms so that you will not even recognize it."[10] He distrusted the sentimentalists because, in his judgment, they were cold rationalists underneath. "The men of our time," he wrote, using a startling image, "have hearts like stone and soft entrails. The earth will belong tomorrow, as it belonged after the Flood, to soft-bodied monsters." "And who knows, it is perhaps the rationalist, hard-hearted planner he had in mind when, to a question of Gaston Picard in 1926, he answered, "I have a good enough impression of the devil when I picture him as an idealist who, in order to take in the imbeciles, baptizes with words from the Gospels the obscene forces which will tomorrow bathe the world in fire and blood."[12]

Naturally, God is no dupe of the Pharisee who today uses social justice as a sort of alibi for his own dry conscience. This is the point on which Bernanos parted company with political parties that have an officially Christian inspiration and Vatican contacts. For him it was of capital importance *that the Gospels should not be equated with a document of "social conscious-ness"* which became now, after the war, a fashionable thought among *bien-pensant* academicians, elegant ladies and conserva-tive politicians. Not that he did not recognize the Gospels' social concern; but he knew that *Christ's message went much farther than the problem of adequate wages and collective bar-gaining.*[13].

There are people who easily detect fallacies in *reasoning;* Bernanos' temperament was such that he always sensed the flaw and duplicity in *feelings* and stressed what was absent from them; before the war, he had called upon the bourgeoisie to understand the plight of the worker in terms of the bread he could or could not buy for his family; after the war, when the subject became fashionable and parties on Left and Right began to vie with each other for the workers' votes, Bernanos insisted that the spiritual bread should not be ignored. He wanted to reverse the order of progress and begin the fight for social reforms not with a de-Christianized "industrious animal," but with the Gospels. Man should first be reshaped by spiritual forces, not by the material environment.

"The Christian Democrats," Bernanos wrote, "have always seemed to me the extreme rear-guard, not to say the stragglers of the Marxist tribe, on march towards the promised land." It is true, he said, that the M.R.P., for example, was the slowest vehicle on the road to Marxism, but even if the poor swimmer keeps to the edge of the water and catches every root and shrub to be delayed, the river carries him towards the same ocean as the bold swimmer in the middle of the current.

He did not distinguish, therefore, or distinguished only very loosely, among the various tendencies within this movement for the reconciliation of democracy and socialism with Catholic doctrine. For him the Christian democrats of the Italian type, the M.R.P. and the *Catholiques de gauche*, the progressives and the Marxists among Catholics were of identical color. Of course, he went much further than that: "Why should we oppose liberalism to Marxism," he asked, "since they are but two aspects of the same surrender of man to his destiny?"[14] For Frenchmen and for Europeans to dwell upon the subtleties of which socio-economic system they should adhere to, was, in his eyes, a gratuitous exercise: ideologies are only the intellectual masks of the real forces in the world, and these forces tend anyway towards reconciliation, thus outflanking all the ideologies. "Every thinking man has understood that America and Russia wage an economic rather than an ideological battle . . . Russia strives more and more to create a type of worker as productive as that of Detroit. And the unionized worker of Detroit, or the farmworker of America's large co-operatives is not so different from the Stalingrad worker or the peasant of the kolkhoze."[15]

It would seem that, between 1945 and his death three years later, Bernanos advocated a position which drew him nearer his earlier-held views than to his post-Majorcan period. More plainly, he seemed to re-adopt the uncompromising attitude—usually identified as "rightist"—before the modern world and its dangers. The truth, however, is not quite so simple; for one thing, we have seen that Bernanos consciously chose to point out threats—to France, to freedom, to civilization, to the inner man—rather than acknowledge gains: thus, after the war when peoples' and governments' attention was turning towards the material aspects of the social problem, his interest moved further, and he became interested in the conditions of mankind's spiritual survival. This does not mean that the first issue for which he had conducted such a courageous campaign in *Les Grands Cimetières* when it was unpopular to do so, disappeared from the circle of his preoccupations; it meant, rather, that as a man of honor and of restless intellect, he preferred to use his weapons against an enemy which seemed to him now by far the deadliest. This was in harmony with his conception of the Christian knight; there are many, he wrote during the war, who cannot or dare not write the truth. "I can and dare. I might as well turn towards my own person the incomprehensions, the rancors, the hatreds which could harm others. As I expect nothing from anybody, these things have no power over me."[16]

For another thing, by launching a violent attack against the dehumanization of man and society, Bernanos merely joined those social philosophers who since Tocqueville have had to adopt a "rightist" vocabulary in their criticism of leftist, progressive ideology and the gigantism it advocates. It is not that Bernanos rediscovered, after the war, the virtues of the Maurrassian school, but that western civilization needs to be reminded of its heritage, tradition and sanity. Concerning these truths, Bernanos did not invent a new theory or offer immediately applicable remedies. Ortega, Jaspers, Toynbee, Guardini and many other critics of mass-man and mass-civilization are more systematic thinkers than he was. But perhaps none understood so completely *from the inside* the plight of modern man and the dangers which threaten him, none had his courage to sound the alarm as he did, and certainly none had that absolutely authentic Christian vision of things which elevates Bernanos' criticism to the supernatural level, the level on which the curé of Ambricourt moved with the assurance of the innocent.[17]

Bernanos, then, remained true to himself when he joined none of the parties of the Fourth Republic but continued as a solitary man, between Left and Right, concentrating on the defense of man. But he was not categorically hostile to ideologies; in fact, he seems to have understood that in the coming world, where uniformity of thought will be spread by great empires and by all sorts of technical instruments, ideologies may express the diversity of opinions and may place obstacles in the way of the all-powerful State. His remarks concerning the similarity of purpose between the United States and Soviet Russia and the cooling-off of their respective ideological commitments are not to be interpreted as an expression of satisfaction but as a signal of danger. In one of his war-time allocutions to "French youth," he said: "It is good that we should have in our country socialists, communists, royalists and anarchists— provided they are sincere and provided they end the rule of conservatives."[18] And conservatives, in his eyes, were people who conserve nothing except their interests, who favor, under all circumstances, the status quo, whether of the Left or Right and who hold as self-evident truth the primacy of the economic order.

TOTAL EQUALITY AND TOTAL SERVITUDE

His preference for the free play of ideologies over the paternalism of Vichy is not a correct indication of his views on democracy, the parliamentary type of government and politics as the monopoly of parties. This issue has not been settled; the Sibylline statements of Bernanos are apt to provoke controversy among his commentators, and his whole career, as an independent man with strongly but often vaguely formulated writings marking the important turning points, leaves him open to partisan interpretations. Thus the present French Right, the intellectual descendants of Maurras, claim Bernanos as one of them, although they admit that he had many a *coup de tête* contrary to orthodoxy. They, in turn, accuse the representatives of leftist Catholicism of trying to tie Bernanos to democratic ideology and Christian progressivism. The fact that Bernanos had entrusted Albert Béguin, late editor of *Esprit*, with the task of editing his unpublished manuscripts, has earned Béguin periodic attacks by those for whom Bernanos remains the *camelot du roi* and member of the *Action Française*.

Without trying to settle the issue between leftist and rightist claimants to the Bernanosian political heritage, we may nevertheless indicate the unquestionably basic ideas of Bernanos on these matters.

Gaëtan Picon argues that a man with Bernanos' generous soul and vision, "ought to have accepted the democratic system."[19] The difficulty is that Picon speaks of democracy in such vague and sentimental terms and equates it with such splendid virtues that these in themselves would be enough to repel the man they were supposed to persuade. Picon then makes the mistake of thinking that Bernanos, after his break with the *Action Française* and particularly in his last years, moved closer to the tradition of the Revolution than to the tradition of Monarchy and nationalism. He quotes Bernanos as having understood that France is not represented by Renan and Maurras but by Michelet and Hugo, that is, the two nineteenth-century archpriests of democracy and popular emancipation.

But although the mature Bernanos detached himself completely from Maurras and his "integral nationalism," he also voiced his disagreement with the "philosophical conceptions of Hugo and Michelet" and with the entire Revolution subsequent to 1789; only the events of the latter year, he wrote, "belong still to the France of the Old Regime, to Old France."[20] It is also true, as Picon reminds us, that Bernanos ended by admiring the France of the radical Clemenceau, and he admired especially Clemenceau himself who proved to be so much more virile, strong-fisted and uncompromisingly patriotic than anybody from the political personnel either of the declining Third Republic or Vichy. But this only proves that Bernanos was not so narrowly partisan as Maurras; he was prepared to give his due to any Frenchman and its due to any movement if they displayed the features which, in his eyes, characterized authentic patriotism: vitality, and spirit of sacrifice. It is not "democracy" that Saint Louis, Joan of Arc, Henri IV, Drumont, Clemenceau and de Gaulle held in common, but their concern for the safety, the well-being and the greatness of France.[21]

Bernanos accepted the Revolution only insofar as it had not disrupted the historic continuity of the country. "I am a man of the old France," he wrote in his *Lettre aux Anglais*, "or, to put it more simply, of France, for a thousand years of history are not to be wiped out by a hundred-and-fifty years of wretched fumbling. Old France is still alive in the France of today. It is merely a matter of having the will to recognize it. I do."[22]

That "wretched fumbling" had been a product of the Revolution: instead of liberating man, the Revolution had strengthened the State, placed it above the law and subordinated the citizen to the community. Modern totalitarianism had its origin in the Jacobin revolution of 1793. "Compulsory military service," Bernanos noted, "has been a real benefit for the State; on the other hand, the vote in the hands of the impoverished individual who became the Nation's property is only an illusion."[23] The King was deprived of his authority, and in him the *petit peuple* lost their only support. And they lost it for the benefit of middle class of *parvenus*, enriched through enormously profitable supplies to the army, the pillage of the emigrés' property and large-scale financial speculations which preceded and followed the Reign of Terror. After that, the members of the Convention, themselves enriched bourgeois, determined to hold on to their illegally acquired wealth and threw themselves into the arms of Napoleon, expecting protection just as the bourgeoisie of 1940 expected protection from Pétain.

Now it was clear to Bernanos that in the historical-political order (he recognized a supernatural order too) democracy has had two sources: the capitalistic system and the French Revolution. His criticism of capitalism is not original and, as pointed out, he repeatedly referred to the mechanical inventions of eighteenth-century England as the upsetter of a better or at least more humanly dimensioned world. Instinctively he rejected the capitalistic mentality, which he associated, like other rightist thinkers, with the narrow-mindedness of the small *commerçant*, the financial scandals of the early Third Republic and the mass-production lines of American industry. Under the collective name of "capitalism," he then understood the profit-mentality, the rejection and isolation of the workers, the huge, impersonal factories. His reasoning, even his vocabulary, is a mixture of Proudhonian and Marxist critique, but, generally, on the economic issue he was inclined to reason with his heart more than with his mind.

Naturally, Bernanos could not separate the problem of capitalism from that of democracy. "Unfortunately, experience seems to demonstrate that the democracies have only been a phase in the evolution of the capitalist society which had destroyed Christian society."[24] He even went so far as to say (with the Marxists) that democracy is the political expression of capitalism, and so its features are the very opposite of aristocratic and heroic virtues. Democracy was for him the reign of mediocrity and of the manipulated masses, the rule of Number over against the articulate individual. The illusion of the vote and the depersonalized factory worker (again a Marxist image) stand to democracy as the structured society and its well-understood rights and obligations stand to the old order. "The law of Democracy," he had written in *La Grande Peur des Bien-Pensants*, "has nothing exalting about it: it is the expression of majority will, that is the expression of a necessity."[25] In fact, Bernanos felt that democracy is intrinsically evil. In spite of its libertarian slogans, themselves the expression of a stage of capitalist growth, expansion and optimism, it opposes freedom and hands the citizen over to the State—again according to an inherent necessity dictated by capitalism's later (that is present) phase. "Even if Communism were to disappear tomorrow, as Hitlerism has disappeared, the modern world would still pursue its evolution towards the regime of world wide control to which even the democracies now seem to be aspiring."[26] Why? Because "democracy means freedom much less than equality, it is infinitely more egalitarian than liberalizing. Every victory of equality appeared to the men around 1900 as a victory for the State . . . To reduce everything to a common denominator facilitates enormously the problem of dictatorships . . . Total equality corresponds to total servitude."[27]

It is evident from these denunciations of the revolutionary principles, capitalism and democracy that Bernanos recognized one urgent task only: resistance to the tyranny now developing throughout the world with the help of the despiritualized individual and the ever-more powerful machines. Often he, too, speaks of revolution, but revolution for him is not the overthrow of a class and the establishment of a so-called classless society in which all would enjoy the irresponsibility of slaves; "The revolution I am announcing will overturn the entire existing order or it will not take place at all . . . The present system will not change the course of its evolution for the good reason that it is no longer evolving; it is merely reorganizing itself with the view of lasting a little longer."[28]

The last sentence is revealing. Although Bernanos' vocabulary could easily be mistaken for leftist extremism or, in its suddenly posed nihilistic-alternative, for the well-known absolute intransigence of the extreme Right, it is clear that he considered the politico-economic history of the last two hundred years—capitalism, liberalism, democracy, fascism, socialism, communism, technocracy—mere variations of the same "system." They were all the skillful yet desperate attempts of the big social beast to appear, periodically, covered with a differently colored hide.

In *La Liberté pour quoi faire?* Bernanos has a striking series of images to describe what, in his view, is actually going on today under the name of "historical transformation" and the "progress of modern civilization"; he likens Europe and the drama of western civilization to a corpse: "It goes without saying that a corpse is essentially an inanimate thing, deprived of a soul. But it is not, for that matter, an inert object. On the contrary, a corpse is all atremble like jelly, shaking, writhing, squirming with a thousand new combinations, the absurd diversity of which leaves traces all over the quivering putrefaction. Yet these histories do not make an *history*. A corpse in a state of decomposition resembles—if a corpse can resemble anything—a world in which the economic consideration has won out decisively over the political, a world which is but a system of irreconcilably antagonistic interests, an equilibrium constantly thrown out of balance . . . A corpse is far less stable than a living body, and if a corpse were able to talk, it would surely brag about the revolution which is going on inside it, about its accelerated evolution. . . . The corpse would scorn the living for the latter's relative stability; it would call him a conservative and even a reactionary, for, it must be admitted, a corpse *is* incapable of reacting. . . . The maggots . . . would say that they are involved in a prodigious adventure, the most absolute of adventures, an irreversible experience. And still, it is a history in admirable conformity with dialectical materialism. There is no room for freedom in it in any form whatever, its determinism is absolute. The error of the maggots, as long as they feed on the corpse, is that they take liquidation for history."[29]

LEFT OR RIGHT? THE PEOPLE'S TRADITION

Can one tell with certainty whether Bernanos was a man of the Right or of the Left? The fact that both claim him, and rather the extremists of the two camps, indicates that it is difficult to conclude but also that it would be important to do so. I have said—and we shall see this in the next chapter more fully— that the tone and the vocabulary of his general denunciation of the modern world is "rightist," just as are the tone and vocabulary of those important contemporary social philosophers and nineteenth-century sages whom we now tend to rehabilitate and bring into light from the shadow where various progressive doctrines had relegated them—Tocqueville, Lord Acton, Bagehot, for example.

The statements of Bernanos himself often leave us in doubt, but the position and reputation he had created for himself are rather clear-cut: he was alike distrusted by both camps. Referring to the 1930's, he noted in July 1943: "Between the rightist press, paid by the enemy, written by academicians and blessed by the archbishops, and the leftist press, on the Kremlin's payroll but less rich and less powerful, we were no more than a handful. The Tartufes of the Right did not forgive us for telling the truth, and the Tartufes of the Left reproached us bitterly for telling it from A to Z. Oh! we were then neither forbidden, nor censored. But we saw the newspapers and magazines shut their doors to us, while the editors, terrorized and fearing a boycott, hesitated to print our writings."[30]

After the skirmish with Maurras and Daudet, one can see that Bernanos finally assumed, with much more freedom than before, his basic eclecticism as far as French history, tradition and destiny are concerned. He trusted his own instinct to tell him what men and what forces had been working for the greatness of France and which ones against her. Thus his personal pantheon of great Frenchmen included, as we have seen, Drumont and Clemenceau (who were mortal enemies), Balzac and Zola, Poincaré and Jaurès. France was his only system of reference. Of his earlier "integral nationalism" he preserved only a few elements: his fidelity to the monarchy, his patriotism and his faith in God, which, in one of its aspects, is also a venerable tradition of France, the eldest daughter of the Church and thus the first Catholic nation in history.

"I am neither of the Left nor of the Right," Bernanos wrote from Brazil, "and if I speak of myself as a royalist and a Christian, I do not thereby join any party. I only wish to assert my loyalty to my people's double tradition, and first of all to God Who was good enough to make me a Christian and a Frenchman."[31] To be on the Left or on the Right did not make sense to him once it became apparent that the contest between the two was taking place at the expense of the entire nation.* Was there such a thing as being right before history? Who was a greater statesman and a truer patriot, the radical Clemenceau or the aristocratic Lyautey? And a more dangerous traitor, Doriot or Thorez? Characteristically, he concluded that there are "imbeciles" on both sides: "Have you understood, blockheads"? he asked. "For fifty years and under such labels as progressives, opportunists, liberals, democrats, patriots, nationalists,

---

* Luc Estang, one of Bernanos' biographers and trusted friends, reaches the same divided conclusion on the question of whether Bernanos belonged to the Right or to the Left. "Bernanos is neither a leftist, nor a rightist. Leaning towards the Left, he believes in generosity towards the people, but refuses to degrade himself by flattering it. A man of old France, he believes in hierarchy. Leaning towards the Right, he rejects the bourgeois spirit favorable to Fascism, and shows, by contrast, the man of the old regime with his Catholic conscience, monarchist heart and mind, and republican temperament." *Présence de Bernanos* (Plon, 1947).

behind all kind of leaders, you have been losing on every card and miserably failing in every enterprise."[32]

If Bernanos belongs to the traditional Right by his royalism, his preference for a hierarchically organized society, his adherence to the principle of authority and his contempt for democracy, he reacted in the manner of a leftist to the Franquist enterprise, to Munich, to Vichy and Pétain. If, with his insistence on social justice and charity and on the duty of the Church towards the victims of capitalism, he came close to the Christian Socialists whom he otherwise rejected, he did not indulge in sentimentalism concerning the "revolution from below": he had only scorn for the progressive intellectuals, Catholic or Voltairean, who believed in the special virtues of the lower classes and in the inherent humanism of the proletariat.

When "Caliban's revolution breaks out," he addressed himself to the rationalist Jean Guéhénno in *Le Crépuscule des vieux*, "I imagine you will want to put in a word, standing among the shirtsleeved men, for a humanism of labor and for culture. But the fellows will be more interested, just then, in pillaging and shooting. M. Guéhénno is hoping that Caliban will wait until the intellectuals complete their discussions and elaborate an ethics of the working class. But the question is, will Caliban wait"?[33]

NOTES

1. *La Liberté pour quoi faire?*, p. 207.
2. Quoted in *Bulletin*, No. 22, April 1955.
3. Em. Mounier, "Un surnaturalisme historique," essay in *L'Espoir des deséspérés* (Ed. du Seuil, 1953), p. 209.
4. *Lettre aux Anglais*, p. 185.
5. *La Liberté pour quoi faire?*, p. 40.
6. "Nous sommes en guerre," article in *Carrefour*, July 16, 1947.

7. *Tradition of Freedom*, p. 163.
8. *La Liberté pour quoi faire?*, p. 86.
9. *Les Grands Cimetières sous la lune*, p. 24.
10. *Dans l'amitié de Léon Bloy*, p. XVIII.
11. *Les Grands Cimetières sous la lune*, p. 26.
12. Quoted in *Bulletin*, No. 6, June 1951.
13. On the other hand, he was very much aware of the tendency in certain Catholic circles to conceive the function of religion and Church as a bulwark of property owners and conservatives. "We know," he wrote from Brazil, "that many Christians . . . are inclined to believe that Christ died only for the safety of ownership, the prestige of high officials, and the stability of governments." "Chrétienté française," in *Ecrits de Combat*, p. 35.
14. *La Liberté pour quoi faire?*, p. 235.
15. *Ibid.*, p. 63.
16. *Le Chemin de la Croix-des-Ames*, I, p. 129.—This extreme independence was compatible with a high degree of modesty. Bernanos understood all along that part of his literary success was due to the fact that ultra-conservative circles hoped to make of him a prestigious ally and an influential mouthpiece. This is what he wrote to a Canadian religious in 1940: "Many of those whom I denounce . . . pretend to serve the same cause as I, they were reading my books and praised them publicly. The fact is that they thought I was interested, as they were, in the conservation of the prestige of certain worthies. . . . But in my eyes their social prestige and positions count for nothing." "Lettre à une religieuse canadienne," in *Ecrits de Combat*, p. 14.
17. Bernanos' views on modern man and his civilization will be discussed in Chapter Seven.
18. Quoted in *Bulletin*, No. 23, May 1955.
19. *Georges Bernanos, loc. cit.*, p. 194.
20. *Écrits de Combat*, p. 48.
21. There is a moving statement in one of Bernanos' short contributions to the wartime French bulletin, *Pour la France libre*, published in Buenos Aires. It shows great comprehension of positions antagonistic to his own, against which he fought all

his life. Under the stress of common danger, he was willing to make the difficult conciliatory gesture: "I have never been a republican," he wrote, "but now I understand what this word represented—rightly or wrongly—to thousands of people who had placed their faith and pride in it. There are many other such nouns which divide us when they ought to forge our unity." The article, under the same name as the bulletin itself, "Pour la France libre," is reprinted in *Ecrits de Combat*, p. 28.

22. Quoted in *Plea for Liberty*, p. 48.
23. *Le Chemin de la Croix-des-Âmes*, II, p. 6.
24. From an interview given to the newspaper *A Noite*, October 1938.
25. *La Grande Peur des Bien-Pensants*, p. 432.
26. *Last Essays*, p. 83.
27. *La Liberté pour quoi faire?*, p. 98.—This process will be further analyzed in Chapter Seven.
28. *Tradition of Freedom*, p. 19.
29. *La Liberté pour quoi faire?*, pp. 192–3.
30. *Le Chemin de la Croix-des-Âmes*, p. 354.
31. *Ibid.*, I, p. 51.
32. *Les Grands Cimetières sous la lune*, p. 130.
33. *Le Crépuscule des vieux.*

7   "A Touchstone of Christianity"

In a letter to Dom Besse, in 1919, Bernanos had noted: "Writing, for me, is the condition of my moral life." Whoever is willing to penetrate his world, the inner climate of his novels and of his polemical writings, must be struck by the incredible moral and spiritual tension which is the rule there and which reveals the truth of his statement. But moral life is not merely an individual affair: it must have the human universe as the atmosphere in which it is immersed, with which it creatively communicates. Bernanos labored passionately to sustain the moral condition of the world, and this labor he considered a challenge for each man.

We would not understand anything of his career as a writer if we ignored this capital point. Bernanos was not a pale intellectual, content to register events and distill from them some far-fetched conclusions, but a man bodily and spiritually living in this world, identifying himself *absolutely* with its condition, *viscerally* reacting to its progression, to the risks and dangers it runs, to the signs of its cure and redemption. Bernanos, like the curé of Ambricourt, *divines* the world and people in it, he knows them with the artist's intuition, but even more with a certain supernatural knowledge which penetrates swiftly—arrow-like—and comes to grips with the essential.

Such a view of the world is only given to those who are supernaturally interested in it, that is, in its salvation. If Ber-

nanos' views are often baffling and seem frequently irrelevant—
"he does not conclude" was people's verdict at his post-war
lectures—it is because he does not appear in the guise of an
expert: historian, sociologist, politician—not even in the garb
of a philosopher. Rather, he is one of us—and I do not mean
an "average man"—he probes our condition from within, follows the inner wayfarer in his peregrination, sometimes ver-
bose, sometimes losing the main thread of the dialogue he con-
ducts, but always relevant about the one palpitating subject:
man as he is underneath systems, interests, slogans, poses.

The proof of the tremendous seriousness with which Bernanos looked at the world is that he knew the most atrocious of
temptations that can assail a Christian. "The demon of my heart
often asks—'what is the use?' " he remarked in *Les Grands
Cimetières,* and Professor Lima tells me that in their last conversation in Brazil, Bernanos echoed these words again, affirm-
ing that all hope for saving modern man must be given up.
This was not to be his last word, and the abbé Pézeril was in
his right to call him, in a magnificent funeral oration, "a touchstone of Christianity," *a man of hope.* Bernanos himself was
careful to distinguish between hope and optimism, indicating
that the former is a virtue, "a basic determination of the soul,"
while optimism is "false hope, for the use of cowards and
imbeciles."[1] In a most telling phrase, he defined the highest form
of hope as "despair overcome" (*désespoir surmonté*), putting
thus into a formula the profoundest secret of his heart.

This is to say that he considered the world and its spiritual
condition vital, so vital, in fact, that he was tempted—this is the
meaning of his quoted words—to give himself up in despair
over its disease. The Christian, it is true, lives *beyond* this world,
in the expectation of another; but his hope must find an object
here on earth too, otherwise his faith becomes formalistic,
selfish and distorted. Who can know the inner combat in which
Bernanos engaged his demon?

THE MACHINE PARADISE

When he returned from Brazil and established himself in France, it was with an enlarged sphere of interest and horizon that Bernanos set to work. His central preoccupations had remained the same: the saint among dry souls, the human person among robots, the victims surrounded by exploiters of all kinds. But new themes were now embroidered on the original fabric: the problem of man's freedom on an increasingly mechanized and organized planet, the struggle of the inner man against the reflexes imposed on him by technology, the fundamental paganism of the modern State.

If France had formed the exclusive frame of reference of Bernanos' writings before the war, his newly made acquaintance with another continent and civilization prompted him, after 1945, to focus his interest on global developments. Indeed, in comparison to the interlocking ties of the whole of western civilization—so dramatically demonstrated by the war—France, even Europe, seemed now small and limited, although by no means less important and more negligible. But this new perspective imposed itself on Bernanos as on so many others. His relative proximity, during the Brazilian stay, to the United States, then the new foundations of South American life and civilization, gave him better instruments to judge the old continent and a better sense of proportion for observing the conflict between old and new.

By civilization Bernanos meant the spirit which informs an age, underlies the reflexes of the people, sets their goals and organizes the web of their relationships. More than that, "a civilization is a compromise between what is good and what is evil in man, a defense system against his instincts."[2] This idea brings to mind the concept of equilibrium, served, consciously and unconsciously, by all the forces of which a civilization consists: individuals and the State, the interests of the person and those of the collectivity, freedom and law, progress and tradition. This tension is a fact of life which the Catholic concept of man had incorporated and further refined by the demands it made on the individual. Thus Christian civilization and all those which have preceded it, as well as the "European" civilization which has followed without breaking its organic ties with it, have formed themselves on the same image.

The emergence of the machine has broken this continuity and has ushered in a crisis not only of the present civilization, but of civilization in general. Why is a technical civilization a denial of the very principles which have governed so far the co-existence of men and their covenant with God?

One of the most searching Catholic answers to this question is given by Romano Guardini. In *The End of the Modern World*, Father Guardini contrasts the classical-medieval worldview in which man was a servant of Creation, with the post-Renaissance centuries and their exaltation of man as a master of nature. He then proceeds to show how modern man has been driven to ride technology (as the unhappy hunter rides the tiger in the Chinese tale) which he cannot tame. The more thorough his technological domination over nature, the less he can avoid constructing a new order of things, quasi-independent of nature, but so coherent and so self-sufficient as to constitute a new nature, as it were. In this artificial world, "the crucial events of life—conception, birth, sickness and death—have lost their mystery. They have become biological or social phenomena dealt with by science or by a series of techniques." "Human nature is withering beneath the destructive hands of modernity"; the alienated man is thus born, no longer interested in his universe existentially, with his mind and heart and senses, but bent upon acquiring power; the tragedy of his present condition is that "while gaining infinite scope for movement, man is losing his own position in the realm of being."[3]

Guardini locates the point of no return, not in the materialistic nineteenth century when "technology developed only slowly at the hands of a non-technologized mentality," but in the recent decades. This diagnosis is correct and important: from Descartes to Renan, from Bacon to H. G. Wells, mastery over nature and the happiness of mankind were proudly flown together on the flag of Utopia. Only very near to us in time have technology and mechano-human manipulative devices entered upon an unholy alliance in which the line of separation between the human being and his tools is not always and not clearly distinguishable.

This does not mean that the machine is in itself innocent. Machines are no more tools, Bernanos writes, because they cannot be owned and managed by the individual worker. They require teamwork and their very operation imposes a distance between the manipulators and their products. The theme of the production line often comes up in Bernanos' war-time and post-war writings; yet he recognizes that technological mentality is not merely the *product* of the machine, it is also the *symptom* of a society losing its natural reflexes. He would have agreed with Guardini that the process had started around the beginning of the century; around 1900, the European states still had a human appearance; they lined up behind a human figure, the Tsar, the Emperor, the President of the Republic. People cherished the State because they found in it either the conditions of their prosperity and personal expansion, or, at least, the promise of these things. Every conquest of the State was chalked up for the cause of freedom, order and social peace, no matter how distant in many cases. Nobody noticed (except a Dostoievsky, a Nietzsche, a Lord Acton) that the "humanity" of the state was decreasing and that a huge bureaucratic apparatus would receive the heritage thus relinquished. The World War, post-war upheavals and revolutions, unemployment, the emergence of mass-parties slowly forced the State to abdicate, "not in favor of the 'masses' which, on the contrary, became more defenseless, but for the benefit of a small aristocracy of engineers and policemen."[4]

This development could not have been foreseen. "Suppose,"

Bernanos writes, "that one asked an educated man in the thirteenth, fifteenth or even the seventeenth century, what his idea of the future society was?—He would have answered right away that this civilization will be peaceful, at once very close to nature and prodigiously refined, cultured . . . Millions had been preparing this kind of world. Today we understand their error: the invasion of machines has taken our society by surprise, so that it collapsed under the weight. This is because such an invasion had never been envisaged."[5]

Man succumbed to this invasion because he took his liberty for granted and was unwilling to pay a continued price for it. Freedom was anyway taken to be synonymous with the rule of man, the preparation of the earthly paradise; whatever helped to bring it about—and the machine seemed to be the most powerful among the instruments of happiness—was blessed by the citizen who, moreover, entertained the illusion that, through the means of democracy, he had an effective control on this development and over his own destiny. As long as this was only an image, a dream, the trap laid by the machine was not noticed. The image and the dream were, in fact, the sentimental aspects of an ideology, the ideology of progress, which acted as a stimulant and was, therefore, a beneficial force.

The machine has quickly put an end to this honeymoon mood between man and his planet, because it presented its own intolerant conditions, its own logic and its own image of happiness, that is, efficiency. It represents a tremendous force since it is a mirage of wealth and power, the mechanical embodiment of spirits from ancient folktales, serving man's appetites and serving them here, now, and in fantastic proportions. Compared to the machine nothing else is important; even the ideological vehicle which had facilitated its conquest is dismissed; "every day brings us new proof," Bernanos remarked, "that the age of ideologies is long passed, in New York as well as in Moscow or in London. We see the British imperial democracy, the American plutocratic democracy, and the Marxist Empire walk, if not hand in hand, at least towards the same goal . . . that is, towards maintaining a system inside which they all have acquired wealth and power."[6]

The age of ideologies may be considered as a sort of last stop before the "machine paradise to which we shall arrive in a state of degradation, like beasts." Even the ideologies and their conflicts had been preferable to the universal orthodoxy of machine-civilization when, in the name of efficiency and mechanical perfection, the dreariest of all tyrannies will establish itself. As a Christian, he knew that perfection is not of this world, and that for human beings to claim it is the surest sign of beastliness and Mammon worship.

The ideologies promised *freedom* and *happiness;* can machine-civilization, which is their heir, be counted upon to usher in their reign?

Freedom, in its only understood, that is, collective form, today is known as democracy. Needless to say, Bernanos never counted himself among the democrats; in his judgment, this system was as mechancial as many other aspects of the modern world, and, moreover, it was an irrational way of taking a guess at what the best policy might be under given circumstances. The Gallup-poll and various other opinion-gathering procedures, further caricatural refinements of the democratic principle, support unwittingly Bernanos' skeptical attitude. But let us admit, he says, that modern man, conditioned to the *democratic* ways, has become also enamored of *technology:* can he have both? Can he vote for this or that technician, as he presumed he could for this or that politician?

First of all, he has no competence to judge so-called experts and to choose among them. The very terms "technology" and "technologue" indicate that this domain is beyond the natural understanding and common sense of the citizen and that its extent may only be measured by other technologues. In the

second place, in view of the fact that "modern society will increasingly be an aggregation of technical problems which have
to be solved," everything, from the formulation of the problem
to the blueprinting of the solution and the calculation of its cost
—in money, time, work, human sacrifice—will be strictly
within the expert's competence. "Do you then imagine," Bernanos asks, "that the working of those thousand and one wheels,
each dependent on the other and running faster than lightning,
will wait on the convenience of the honest fellows who come
together at electoral meetings to cheer this or that parliamentary program . . . Technique's every step forward is a
step away from the Democracy that was the old-time worker's
dream."[7]

But of course the disappearance or formalization of democracy is not all. Freedom, under various other forms, cannot
be preserved under a mechanical civilization. Chateaubriand,
to mention only one, had foreseen, a hundred years before
Bernanos, the coming loss of privacy and the decreasing importance of the individual. He had written, in the epilogue to his
Mémories d'Outre-tombe: "The folly of the age is to achieve
the unity of the peoples while turning the whole species into a
single unit. Granted. But while we are acquiring these general
faculties, is not a whole chain of private feelings in danger of
perishing?" Chateaubriand, a child of the individualistic eight-
eenth century, was confronted only by powerless ideologues
of the type of Saint-Simon and Comte and dreaming social
prophets like Michelet; but Bernanos and ourselves, his contemporaries, have measured the progress of a totalitarianism
of a different sort, under dictatorships as well as under mass-
democracy; we risk no longer merely to lose "a chain of private
feelings" in a world where people are conditioned daily to have
identical reactions and hysterias, but the complete loss of our
individuality in most of its manifestations.

"The disciplines imposed by technique have slowly ruined,
or at least considerably weakened the reflexes of the individual

against the collectivity", wrote Bernanos.[8] We must bear in mind that this was, for him, not a mere historical accident, reparable or irreparable, but a sin against God's most precious gift. Political, social and intellectual freedom are, after all, aspects of the creature's strongest link to the Creator, the source of his personality and the stamp of his dignity. To sign it away is not merely to re-enact the drama of Faust, but a sure indication of an inner unbalance, the severance of roots, after which there is only the petrification of the soul and of the faculties it commands and vivifies. This is why Bernanos can say that "one cannot understand the least thing about modern civilization if one does not first realize that it is a universal conspiracy to destroy the inner life";[9] and why he refers, a few pages further, to machine civilization as a "cancer," "a profound, aberrant crisis, a deviation, a perversion of human energy."[10]

However, for many modern thinkers *happiness* is still achievable in the service of the State, the collectivity, or even outside them; and it is possible even without the breath of *freedom* to enliven it. Immense forces crush the individual, they say, and in order to struggle effectively against them, the collectivity alone can and must be counted upon. It is therefore in the interest of the individual, it is indeed the very meaning of his freedom, that he should alienate this freedom—temporarily or forever—and subordinate himself to community-set aims. The result will be a *new happiness*, stripped of the egoistic features of the old, the happiness of public immersion, of being part of the whole, of being absorbed in the *Nirvana of togetherness*.

This new concept of happiness, related to technological progress, is guaranteed by the State. The State uses the machine and imposes the equality and the organization which the forces liberated by the machine require if they are to be prevented from running wild. Mechanical perfection will, indeed, emancipate the worker from everyday drudgery, but will also relocate him to bureaucratic posts where he will no more understand the meaning of his activity than on the assembly line. In addition, it is highly doubtful that his relationship to his superiors will improve; the same distance as before will be maintained between the unskilled worker or clerk, displaced by the machine, and the few thousand specialists who will keep his destiny in their hands. The argument that the masses, freed from the most painful type of manual work and physical exertion, will now have enough time for leisure, that they will be more "cultured" and better "informed," is so thoroughly contradicted by the facts we have been witnessing for the past few decades, that it must be relegated to the rubbish heap of other "progressive" dreams.

In several of Bernanos' novels there appears a twentieth-century version of Monsieur Homais, whether as a journalist, a half-educated student or an escaped seminarian; in each case he is not only weak and mediocre, but vicious as well, a creature whose insignificance of intellect is matched only by the insincerity of his soul. Bernanos could never persuade himself that small-time intellectuals are anything but parasites. "What can the world expect of cultural equality?" he asked. "What an illusion to believe in the fraternity of idling intellectuals!"[11] He saw in them, indeed, pale copies of the diabolical figures which Satan in an egalitarian age uses to tempt man by what is most shameful in him. According to Bernanos, as Mounier remarks, the present world does not deserve any prowess on the part of Satan who apportions his efforts by the power of the resistance offered. Mediocre people cannot sin, and are, therefore, not tragic; *their only form of revolt is indifference*.

The most pernicious among modern evils is, then, *mediocrity*. Bernanos who ultimately trusted the individual alone, found the latter's indifference and lack of resistance far more dangerous than the more awesome forms of modern techniques of oppression. The mediocre and indifferent ones are, by definition, indistinguishable from each other, since all they aspire to achieve is to be part of the whole, to let things take their course, to be one among the many. In them the soul is dead, their existence consists of elementary reactions to animal needs. The only function they fulfill in society is *to be counted*—to form the units of statistics, to constitute the mass. "A world dominated by Force is an abominable world," Bernanos exclaimed, "but a world dominated by Number is ignoble. Force sooner or later becomes a challenge and invites revolt. It calls for heroes and martyrs. The abject tyranny of Number is a slow infection which provokes no fever. Number creates a society after its own image, a society of human beings, who are not equal but identical, recognizable only by their fingerprints."[12]

How could one speak of happiness in their case, provided we mean by happiness something worthy of God's creatures? Since they offer no resistance, the gigantic forces of the age pass through them and determine their fate as well as their concept of happiness. These forces, that is, the technicians who manipulate them, dispose of enormous means to carry out their plans and transform mankind into a "colony of industrious animals." If work itself will become lighter from a strictly physical point of view, the filling of leisure hours will represent real difficulty since the "industrious beast" will be deprived of imagination, real creativity, even of a desire to indulge in anything but the collectively approved forms of entertainment.

Thus Bernanos saw clearly the problem of modern man in industrial mass societies, the problem which is becoming more acute every day: the freedom of empty or half-furnished minds who turn to destruction, nihilism, or the most vulgar and superficial forms of commercial and State-devised distraction. He identified correctly also the personnel moving into the posts vacated by the elite, the "engineers of the soul" as Stalin called them. "Committees of psychologists will argue with committees of moralists and committees of theologians until the citizen's every last indefeasible right will be warranted by half a score of governmental offices, open daily from 9 to 5, excepting, of course, for Sundays and holidays."[13] The only sort of inner life these experts will allow will be "a modest and moderate form of introspection, directed by the doctor and tending to produce an optimistic frame of mind."[14] The last word, after all, will be *happiness* as promised; only it will be the happiness of the unfree, soulless, directed man, working and playing under supervision and reduced to the state of a robot.

THE WARDEN STATE: THE ORDER OF A GRAVEYARD

If human beings turn into robots, so must necessarily the State which is no longer informed by the spirit of freedom; contrary to what one would assume at first glance, the disciplining of robots is a more difficult task than the settling of conflicts among rational and free men. Robots being small wheels in a machinery, the latter must be immensely powerful if it is to work smoothly. Nor can it—that is, the State—be absolutely sure that today's robots might not become tomorrow's rebels, since, after all, not inert matter but human beings are involved in the present historic crisis. As we shall see, Bernanos envisages such a possibility, that is, the revolt of freedom in the desolate cemetery of the machine paradise.

He considered it an irrefutable point that machines, ever larger, more perfect and supremely efficient, must become the monopoly of the State. No legislation, no semblance of private capitalism, no billion-dollar corporations with all their machine-given power and wealth, may remain outside the ubiquitous State, although arrangements may be reached in the form of this or that compromise. Ultimately, however, the machine must work for the State, and the individual owner—insofar as big corporations can at all be called "individual owners"—

becomes, at best, a huge middle man between the State and the public.

Power thus accumulated in the hands of the "warden State" —the name given by Bernanos to the nameless collectivity— can be assimilated into a dictatorship. Not the dictatorship of one man—this has never been the case—but of the party of the Technocrats, far more powerful because more cohesive than a party of ideologues and politicians who, after all, like to interpret ideas and who therefore disagree. The Technocrats do not disagree, at least not on essentials. For them, universal dictatorship is an absolute, short of which they cannot stop because the technocratic mentality, like the machine it copies, tolerates no obstruction, no contradiction to its efficiency.

One can still argue, as the majority of men do, that the technocrats, their technique and power, will exercise control over the material world only; machines take the place of the servant, reduce the hours of work, open so-far unsuspected ways of subduing a hostile nature. These services of technology and science, the argument runs, facilitate rather than obstruct the superior kind of life because they make leisure and culture possible; schools, theatres, libraries, travel and tourism are available to the millions who thereby enrich themselves and prepare for yet higher forms of freedom and the good life.

Bernanos fought this argument with special violence. "Watch out!" he cried, "among all the techniques there is a technique of discipline for which the mere obedience of the past is not satisfactory. Obedience used to be obtained by all kinds of empirical methods, so that one may say that it was less a discipline that a moderate disorder. Technique, on the other hand, will sooner or later insist on forming its own collaborators, who will belong to it body and soul, who will accept without discussion the technical concept of order, life and the reason for living. In a world which is entirely devoted to Efficiency and Production, it is imperative that each citizen, from his birth, should be consecrated to the same gods. Technique cannot be called into question since the solutions it imposes are by definition the most practical."[15]

If it cannot be called into question, much less can it be opposed. The fact that the old forms of aristocratic and monarchic abuses were successfully combatted and destroyed by a militant and meaningful *liberalism*, makes us believe that now, when the descendants of those liberals favor an all-powerful State, we should continue trusting and acclaiming them. But virtuous action in the past represents no guarantee of virtue for the future, much less infallibility. Indeed, it may have been corrupted by its very success. The all-powerful State, with the help of its machines and robots, will tolerate no contradiction and no opposition, even with the liberal label on it. "In proportion as the causes of disorder will double or triple, technique will increase its means of defense and repression tenfold, a hundredfold. Order will be maintained, but it will be the order of a cemetery. It will be maintained in the name of a Society of which only the administrative framework and the police will have survived—a skeleton."[16]

This will be the end; meanwhile, the State grows and expands; it takes care of its citizens and thinks for them. It says: since I do these things for you and plan to do more, why don't you trust me with your freedom? What possible use can you make of liberty? I shall be free for you, I shall be free alone. Thus the Pagan State is conceived, says Bernanos, which is the same thing as the pagan god. "And what will it matter," he adds, "under which name we must adore it—Democracy or Dictatorship?"[17]

THE FREE MAN

Throughout the Bernanosian analysis it is clear that the writer is speaking not only as a citizen, a critic, a Frenchman, a contemporary to fateful events, but first and foremost as a Christian. Characteristically, he called the coming State not a "brave new world", "1984," "post-historic world," "post-western civilization,"—but the *pagan state*. As a Christian, feeling *one* with Christian history and tradition, he knew what the pagan state was and the menace it once represented. In fact, he conceived of the present threat as greater than in the first centuries of Christianity: nobody can say of the first Christians that they were mediocre and that they shunned risks. Today, however, people—and this includes Bernanos' fellow-Catholics—are mediocre, they seek security and the comfort of the soul. The pagan state of the future will be immeasurably stronger than Nero's and Diocletian's had been, and Bernanos knew that it would persecute Christians and free men for the same reasons.

But the modern state is not so much a danger in itself as a means of measuring the corruption of the underlying reality: of the individual and the collectivity. One of Bernanos' recurring themes was the idea that just as the abdication of elites within society makes way for pseudo-elites and ultimately for a generalized wickedness, so, on another plane, the abdication of society itself, its scorn for humanness, is responsible for the cancer-like growth of the State. The images Bernanos uses to express this observation are, again, similar to those he used in the description of the abbé Cénabre; when the abbé's spirtual vocation ran down like a bad clock, there began at once the invasion of moral and corporal degradation; uncleanliness, like maggots on a corpse in another image, attack immediately like an enemy who had been waiting at the gate and who had been kept out only by a constant, unceasing effort and vigilance.

With regard to the progress of evil in the abbé Cénabre, I have used the word "carapace" under which his decomposition remained invisible (except to the abbé Chevance and Chantal). Bernanos used a similar image to paint the new, sinister role of the State. "Human society is in the process of dissolution. Totalitarian organization is to this society in dissolution what wooden or metal braces would be to a body which is rotting away. The braces become more and more rigid, take more and more room in proportion as the body occupies less, until the day when the orthopedic apparatus replaces completely the body which is then reduced to naught."[18] (Let us bear in mind that Bernanos meant mass-democracy no less than Hitlerism and Bolshevism when he spoke of totalitarian regimes.)

Society in a state of putrefaction, the "sclerosis of individual consciences," the "liquidation of history," "spiritual entropy," "man amputated of God," are sources, signs and consequences of the phenomena observed by Bernanos. He did not make these observations systematically, nor did he order them in a logical or historical sequence. The principal virtue of his analysis—and the sureness and depth of his diagnosis—derive from his underlying assimilation of society to the individual, society's sense of freedom and honor to the individual's moral conscience, society's resignation to the individual's despair, its corruption to his turning against God. In short, Bernanos, throughout his social-polemical works, remained a novelist, retaining the novelist's psychological insights, and the novelist, in turn, never ceased to be a Christian. Thus the ultimate answer Bernanos proposes is always a Christian answer: like the curé of Ambricourt and Chantal de Clergerie whose sanctity cuts through the Gordian knot of evil, so the saint, the authentically free man, is to save the world from the tyranny engulfing it.

As we have seen, this does not mean that Bernanos was spared the temptation of despair. I have mentioned his idea that real heroism is hopelessness overcome; the experience must have been familiar to him. His writings show abundantly that he was almost constantly balanced between resignation and hope—so much so that the superficial reader may even accuse him of incoherence. However, this same frequent absence of logical reasoning is proper to all those thinkers whose philosophy is of the existential kind, and who do not seem to be able to decide whether to follow the indications of intelligence or that of faith. For the first tells them that man, once he is engaged in a process of abdication, builds system after system in justification of his preference for un-freedom; while the second reminds them that there is always in man an indestructible residue of spiritual longing by which, and with God's help, he chooses the fullness of life.

This "inconsistency" was the substance of the thought of Pascal, Kierkegaard, Nietzsche and Shestov, to mention only a few, and it received a particular emphasis with Bernanos in whose case the philosophical difficulty was further complicated by an interest in political events and prophecies, the future of France and the fate of western civilization. Thus he is perfectly truthful and consistent when he finds no saving grace for the modern world, and yet puts all his feverish hope into the individual's last stand. "People agree with me," he wrote towards the end of his life, "that this civilization is deceptive and dangerous; they cannot accept the idea that it may be unreformable. They reassure themselves by thinking that man will end up some day by redecorating the interior of this civilization . . . Their error is that they never wonder if the experiment in process could not be followed in spite of man, because of the enormous means it commands."[19]

Yet, there are many texts and passages of his speeches from the same period in which he dismisses any determinism and necessary decline, and points up signs of an unexpected side-street which does not lead to a dead end. Before an audience at the Sorbonne, he advised the students not to think that mankind is "a locomotive launched on its rails" and following an inevitable course; rather, he said, "compare it to a work of art that the artist begins to shape again and again." This comparison is, of course, an old one, for the image of the clay, formless but taking shape under the sculptor's fingers, has been a favorite of believers of all kinds. In Bernanos, it shows, together with and inseparable from the more somber predictions, that in his extreme sensitiveness he registered the progress of every ripple on the ocean of life and tried to guess its final destination.

It is not surprising that he found most ripples expanding in the wrong direction. Again, it was his rational side which suggested to him that once man gives away a parcel of his freedom, he may never reconquer it. In a passage of the *Lettre aux Anglais,* he explains his anguish over the irreversible trend away from the individual: "Man is not made to live alone, and the strayed members of the flock invariably end by coming back to it. Whereas if man one day sacrifices the rights of the Person to some collectivity, he will never find them again, for that collectivity will ceaselessly grow in power and material efficiency . . . You will tell me that the democratic Collectivity will never make any attempt against the sacred rights of the Person. Forgive me, but how can I be sure of any such thing? Why should not the majority tomorrow impose upon me its own moral code if mine stands in the way of its profits?"[20]

Yet, the man of faith provides the answer, namely in the same *Lettre aux Anglais:* "I do not deny," he writes, "that human society seems to evolve towards a kind of universal collectivism, but this is because the forces of defense of the human person are as if struck by stupor. Nevertheless, these forces exist and their reaction will be like a thunderbolt. What is needed to spark it? The passionate will of a few thousand men, free and proud."[21]

Note that these "few thousand men" do not have to form a political elite, in fact they do not have to form a group, a party, a network: they do not have to be linked in any way. Their power of reaction is their "freedom and pride" which would be vague requirements, indeed, if Bernanos had not so often given flesh and bone to these words in his novels and through his own behavior. What he means then is not an organized opposition to the modern world, because he knows, or rather feels with a sure instinct that the most acute danger of this world is, precisely, that in it even freedom must organize, must build a heavy apparatus and finally strengthen the very image of man it means to combat. No, in Bernanos' judgment the Technical State will "have no enemy but *the man who is not like other men*,[22] or, more simply, the man who does not believe in Technique."[23] Why is he a danger to machine-civilization? Because "the modern world is a mechanism with such complicated interlocking parts, that the presence of one single free man exposes it, sooner or later, to a peril similar to that which a planet, miraculously exempt from the laws of gravitation, would create in the solar system."[24] Such free men, Bernanos says on another occasion, using another image, would be "the grains of flint which, because of the ever-present danger they create, use up the zeal of the machinery's engineer and hold in check its appetite."[25]

THE SAINT

Is this free man, hypothetical or actual, a mere *saboteur*, a bitter opponent who finds pleasure, however justified, in placing obstacles in the way of the machine's heavy feet, in delaying the inevitable march of the Technical State? Or is he the Bernanosian *saint*, disposing of an inexhaustible reservoir of fighting spirit, but also of insight and charity, used not for malice and destruction, but for opposing, endlessly, freedom to indolence, love to routine? It is true that, carried away by his famous tempests of fury, Bernanos had frequent moments when he charged, bull-like, all those who seemed to oppose his own version of honesty, good faith and courage; his friends, acquaintances, audiences, interviewers, confessors, all testify that nobody was spared on such occasions: academicians, men of letters, generals, ministers, chiefs of state, political parties, frivolous ladies, prelates were brought up to the eye of the needle, only to find that they could not pass. Back in France, after 1945, he used to declare that the freest man today was the one who refused all participation, because every group, party or interest was selfish and corrupt. But there was another Bernanosian reaction too: once before, Bernanos, we have seen, had referred to the saint "thrown across the path" of modern cynicism and hypocrisy: it was the abbé Donissan in *Under the Sun of Satan* whose lonely and tormented figure was called upon to shock post-war France into a recognition of the devil lurking on sideroads and defying the unwary. In the teeth of a universal danger it is again the saint who will prove himself God's champion.

First, as the Poor and as the Child. Like Léon Bloy, Bernanos understood the profound Christian truth that *poverty* cannot be suppressed only displaced. With other Catholic philosophers, he saw in Marxism a doctrine which humiliates the poor and robs him of his dignity by enrolling him in the proletarian horde and assuming that he lives by bread alone. The colossal system of "changing the world" implies, in his eyes, a ruthless regimentation, the degradation of all higher ambition in view of the supreme recompense: filling the stomach. The poor, he maintained, are jealous of their individuality and do not mean to stand on their hindlegs for a bone. Marxism does not offer them a more dignified life, that is, a recognition and justification of their higher aspirations, but, on the contrary, insists on reducing all men to the level of proletars, by denying their spiritual nature. Marxism, of course, is not alone to blame: industrial capitalism had long before deformed the full image of man and had made of him, through its own angle of vision and interests, the *homo economicus*, Bernanos' (and Tocqueville's) "industrious beast." Marx, opposing the British textile manufacturers and coal mine operators, had fallen into their error.

The Child too is, for Bernanos, a prefiguration of the saint. I have shown, in the first chapter, in what sense his conception of the child is opposed by the modern concept of educators, psychologists and business interests, all of which converge upon the child in order to make of him a small adult, a target of salesmen, researchers and experimenters. These representatives of the modern adult world are impatient to integrate him in the circuit of their own affairs; the child must be made an accomplice and a victim of efficiency, he must serve science and production, he must not be a point at which society becomes incalculable, wastes time, and risks raising a generation indifferent to its own strange predilection for self-harassment.

But the real saint is more than the child and the poor, although he partakes in the virtues of both and also in that special grace that God seems to bestow on them. The role of the saint, a supernatural role, is to serve as a mysterious entity in the divine plan to counter-balance evil. All the physical and spiritual strength of Donissan was needed to stand up to the devil's challenge; the curé of Ambricourt, weak and sickly as he was, wielded fantastic power over those entrusted to him; Chantal, the fragile flower of a day, burned up in her quiet glow the poison of the maniacs and shallow souls around her. The saint who faces the modern world must represent God's interests in a different, yet similar situation; grace must overflow in him so that he may offer himself not on every front, for he is but a limited man, but with the help of that special virtue by which spirit can be infused into an inert body, by which the non-material may be everywhere at once. Bernanos firmly believed that only Christians had a chance to save the modern world: "Christianity divinizes man. Less than that is not enough for the balancing of the enormous advantage that Collectivity has over the Person. If we do not claim membership in the human order, we shall fall under the iron law of the Giant State . . . The triumph of man in this world will be obtained only through a flawless self-discipline."[26]

Bernanos does not speak of the self-discipline of the ascetic and of the monk, although, as the example of the abbé Donissan and of the curé of Ambricourt shows, he justified self-mortification as an offering to God for the sins of others and also as a means of gaining more spiritual authority over them. But the ideal type for him always remained the militant saint—Joan of Arc, Saint Louis—to whom it never occurred to tend his supernatural virtues as some rare flower, but who engages it in the thick of the battle. The saints in his novels are amazingly *robust* spiritually and give themselves with prodigality, never once thinking of sparing their God-given energy. Yet their exceptional qualities are not barriers between them and the rest of the mortals. Since they form the true elite—of the Church and of mankind—there is no limit to their willingness to risk their life and entire being. Hence, they do more rather than less, they are constantly at their task, and do not separate themselves from the others in the knowledge of their apartness. The saints are witnesses that the world is blessed by God and that sanctity is, therefore, not the exceptional but the normal; Mounier rightly remarks that Bernanos has eliminated any rare or sublime quality from his saints: "he pushes them with both hands towards banality and shapes them like very down-to-earth figures. Their task is to be well understood by all."[27]

This saint who is so deeply rooted in the earth, is *in* the world while serving a supernatural plan. But, of course, he has no program, no system. Indeed, he is embarrassed by the fact that others, with mixed respect and suspicion, credit him with superior intelligence and complicated designs. How innocent is Chantal's cry when she is reminded that her presence among her father's strange guests poses problems: "Am I a problem? . . . You too think so? But what problem?"

The misunderstanding is only apparent. The saint, in reality, is simple because his inner being is turned towards the very source of simplicity. It is again Chantal who says: "One ought to be like crystal, like pure water. One ought to be transparent so that God might be seen through us." It is always the others who see a *problem* in the saint's presence because he obstructs their deviousness.

But the misunderstanding and the conflict are, of course, never-ending and manyfold: in the great figures of his novels Bernanos saw not only the heroes of spiritual battles but also true revolutionizers of man's existence. This is why the saints are the best qualified to take up arms in man's defense: they are "fellows who . . . would let themselves be made into mincemeat before giving Caesar anything more than his due."[28] In this way the *saint*—that is, in his relationship to society, the *free man*—assumes two roles, both of which are deliberately left undefined with any precision: one is what we may call the "saboteur," the "flint among the wheels of the machine"; the second is the "resistant," who is irreducible and unassimilable by the technological mentality and by the State.

It must be stressed once more that Bernanos had too clear an insight into the nature of freedom to impose a "pattern of freedom" and a course of action for his saint; the saint is what he is because he is a *man*, that is, literally incalculable to the clumsy machinery that the State uses in its classification of the citizen's inner life and external behavior. This does not mean that his actions are random actions, dictated by whim and deliberate non-conformity; he is rather like Bernanos himself, that is, at peace with his conscience because he follows truth as he sees it.

Also like Bernanos, the "saboteur," the "resistant" is a solitary man; naturally, he is *in* the world, as I have said before, and he freely shoulders the duties accruing to him in society. If he preserves his freedom, it is not in the Gidean sense of "disponibility," of never choosing at the crossroads of life. On the contrary, he has chosen once and for all; his apparent changes measure only the shifts among his fellow-men. But he is a solitary man as opposed to the mass-man of our age. He is the element of freedom which vitiates the social calculus, the one atom whose path cannot be described in advance.

To say that the saint is a saboteur is not to say that he lacks charity and that he finds pleasure in upsetting progress. Of "progress," of course, Bernanos had very definite views and, as can be expected, less than favorable.[29] But precisely because it seemed to him that his fellow-men lost their sane judgment in sacrificing their freedom and life for the ephemeral monsters of progress, he imposed a third mission on his saints: he wanted

them to redeem not only the misguided, but, above all, the evil
guides.

The final proof of Bernanos' perfect grasp of the modern
world—and of his flawless Christianity—is that he identified
the creators of modern civilization—the liquidators and the
human maggots—with the supernaturally *poor* who must be
saved before everybody else. Mounier calls this insistence on
saving the guilty "a desperate invitation to fraternity unto death,
launched to the brother who is blinded by the evil spirit."[30] I
do not think that this appeal of Bernanos was born in despair;
on the contrary, in my view it shows great confidence to make
room for the prodigal brother in the Father's tent. Bernanos
who attacked without respite the "imbeciles," and the greatest
of them all, the builders of Babel, of the earthly paradise, knew
well that their lack of faith was crushing them with the whole
weight of the universe. Only the saints are able to relieve the
burdens of the greatest sinners.

The word "prophet" comes involuntarily to one's mind
when speaking of Bernanos—for several reasons: his *indignation* before the spiritual state of the modern world, his loud and
eloquent *denunciation* of certain people and classes and his
readiness to show the road of a radical regeneration, that is his
forgiveness. These are, however, the qualities of the prophet,
and are not, on every point, reconcilable with those of the
polemicist. As a result, we find Bernanos often guilty of remaining within the sphere of generalities, neglecting the duty
of illustrating the problems he raises, as if the fire of the truth
he proclaims—and with which we agree—were sufficient to
illuminate the unelaborated details of his subject. At other times,
however, the image he uses is so expressive that it replaces, by
itself, a painstaking documentation, and gives us the supreme

satisfaction of seeing, in a flash, from within. Among contemporary French writers perhaps Bergson alone had a similar gift.

Another defect of Bernanos is that he frequently interrupts his discussion in order to pour his wrath on adversaries, after which he grafts yet other issues on the newly-found one: the result is a network of unrelated topics, all brilliant as far as they go, but weakened in persuasive power. Gaëtan Picon aptly remarks that Bernanos conceived his novels as "total expressions"; it is quite clear that he had the same view of his polemical works as well: even when they are intended to focus on one issue, they soon turn into "total expressions" of the writer's world view.

All this followed from the fact—emphasized so many times in this book—that Bernanos remained a novelist even in his polemical writings. But when I say a "novelist," I must give that word an extended meaning, as in the case of a Dostoievsky or a Proust, who were also immersed in their stories as in a concentrated form of life. But while with Dostoievsky and Proust—certainly the latter—the novel was a substitute for life and took precedence over life, Bernanos envisaged the writer's problem the other way around: he was primarily interested in life, and his novels and polemics were two ways of illustrating this interest. Most emphatically he did not write *romans à thèse*, fictional versions of his beliefs and convictions; his fictional characters and the real characters whom he observed, described, analyzed and criticized were, for him, men and women belonging to the same universe; they would have been capable of exchanging roles and continuing to live in the framework either of the novels or of real life.

There are two reasons for this: one is Bernanos' amazing knowledge of the human being, a knowledge which always starts from the deepest depth of the soul. Once his grasp of the inner man is secured, it is relatively easy for him to show everything as following from this inner reality: behavior and words are attached to the soul's secret like a dog, held on leash, to his master. It is this insight that Bernanos trusted under all circumstances, whether observing real life or writing his stories.

The second reason is the identity of the atmosphere that he creates in the novels and in the polemical writings. Even behind and around trivial acts there is drama and tension because, in the Bernanosian view, the soul is always involved and we are never indifferent. Or, if we are, it is a form of Satan's temptation, that is another potential drama. The world of politics, the life of nations, conflicts of class or group interests set the same forces into motion as life on a personal level since nations, classes, even the State and the machine also have souls, are bathed in the atmosphere of sin, perdition and redemption.

This concept of life, fictional *and* real, is faithfully rendered by his style which, in turn, was the exact manifestation of his personality. Stanislas Fumet, who had encouraged his early steps as a writer and helped publish his first novel, wrote of his style: "He conceived of writing as of an attack. Sentences upon sentences, overwhelming, overwhelmed, scintillating; here a zone of obscurity, there a patch of light." To this we may add the observation that he had learned a great deal from Drumont, from Léon Bloy and Péguy, the three men with whom he undoubtedly forms a *group* on several counts. From Drumont he inherited the style of the charging bull, the relentless pursuer of the opponent; from Bloy the apocalyptic visions and vaticinations; and from Péguy the poetry of the soul, expressed in calmly developed images, impressed on the reader (and better still, on the hearer) by means of abundant repetitions like in old epic poems.

These gifts and shortcomings he put in the service of a grand ideal, the regeneration of mankind. No doubt his understanding of the nature of evil—the first condition of such a regeneration—was exceptional: there is no writer today who could compose a scene like the confrontation of the Countess by the curé of Ambricourt on the eve of her death. The same subtlety and forcefulness as were displayed by the curé were

Bernanos' eminent weapons in fighting his own battles against the devil whose ways and strategy he understood with a truly supernatural insight. This is why he forms in us not only a conceptual understanding of the great issues and dramas of this age, but a palpitating reality as well, which makes us shudder and leaves us terror-stricken, or raises us to pity and love, and which, finally, makes it clear why we are part of the world he describes. His images and visions are, of course, magnificent, whether morbid or elevating, hopeful or hellish: but it is the total spiritual comprehension of the world—a catholic comprehension—which makes them so expressive of reality and which, in turn, convinces us of reality's higher dimension: truth.

But how can one speak of truth when Bernanos was a partisan who, all his life, rejected caution and revised his judgments more than once? Yet, the word is not out of place: *truth*, in the sense of an incredibly generous spiritual grasp of things human, and *truth* in the sense of bringing his political understanding up to the level of his charity. I have remarked earlier that we may suspect in Bernanos' inner life some tremendous combats with his demon, the temptation of despair, and that it must have cost him an immense energy to love the "imbeciles," the soul-corrupters, the Pharisees he had detected under so many disguises: the respectable bourgeois, the gullible Machiavellian, the false priest, the soulless technician, the seeker of a spiritual alibi in "social concern." But precisely: the more he understood of the world, the more essential he found that it should be saved without exclusions. There is, when all is said and done, a Tocqueville's political wisdom in him, transfigured by a stronger faith still that we must seek the conditions of *total* regeneration. In spite of his love and admiration of certain forms of the life and images of the past, he ridiculed those who accused him of "medieval" mentality; he lived very much in this world and age, but saw no reason why this age should be exceptional: he understood that in his forsakenness, modern man is even more a child of God, a child calling out—silently and shamefacedly—to his Father.

This generous understanding—again Tocqueville's grasp of the age of democracy and liberalism comes to one's mind—made it possible for Bernanos to evolve from the position of a twentieth-century Drumont to a unique position, without labels, but stamped with the sign of hope. To follow his own distinction: not optimism but hope. Given this humility, the great events of his life—and of his political consciousness—the break with Maurras, the testimony of Majorca, life in Brazil, the shock of the "stolen Resistance" (as victory had been stolen in 1918), all were liberating and deepening experiences, ranged on a continuous line and permeated with the same conviction, the inspiration behind Bernanos' political concern. This conviction is religious in nature because its source is the belief that the saints are capable of saving the more indolent members of the mystical body. Similarly, within society or the nation, the elite must labor for the material and moral well being of the people. Failure in this task is treason, the only guilt Bernanos never seems to forgive because, in his view, it is the point of origin of other sins against the people by an abdicating elite which, nevertheless, clings to the power it does not deserve.

In this respect there is, indeed, little difference between the elite which betrays its mission and the priest who loses his vocation. They display the same symptom: inability to address and guide those who would naturally trust them; the priest drives the penitent to despair, the elite sows confusion among the people. Bernanos' great polemical works: *La Grande Peur des Bien-Pensants, Les Enfants humiliés, Les Grands Cimetières sous la lune, Scandale de la vérité* and his post-1945 articles, are all denunciations of elites which failed in the dialogue in 1871, in 1918, in 1936, in 1940 (Vichy), in 1945 (the Resistance). He remained convinced to the end that the people—*le petit peuple*—would have understood them.

Thus every political experience nourished his substance, and was turned by him into a profound concern. Had he not retained the simplicity of childhood, his preoccupations would have made him a cynic; had he not been a man of absolute faith, they would have overcome him. He escaped these temptations because he never doubted God's mercy; and he never doubted his own vocation: this is why, in Mauriac's parting words, he became, in the last years of his life, "an old molossus with bloodshot eyes, biting at the shins of fat sheep and foolish ewes."

NOTES

1. *La Liberté pour quoi faire?*, p. 15.
2. *Ibid.*, p. 189.
3. Romano Guardini, *The End of the Modern World* (New York: Sheed and Ward, 1956).
4. "Nous sommes en guerre," in *Carrefour*, July 16, 1947. Bernanos means here the State as a traditional entity, as the product of history, the organizer and civilizer of society. We shall see farther on what he thought of the modern State.
5. *La France contre les Robots*, pp. 133–34.
6. *Ibid.*, pp. 24–25.
7. *Tradition of Freedom*, p. 148.
8. *La Liberté pour quoi faire?*, pp. 106–7.
9. *Tradition of Freedom*, p. 105.
10. *Ibid.*, p. 114.
11. *Nous autres, Français*, p. 162.
12. *La France contre les Robots*, pp. 182–183.
13. *Lettre aux Anglais*, p. 183.
14. *Tradition of Freedom*, p. 156.
15. *La France contre les Robots*, pp. 194–195.
16. *Lettre aux Anglais*, p. 154.
17. *Plea for Liberty*, p. 242.
18. "Nous sommes en guerre," in *Carrefour*, July 16, 1947.
19. *Last Essays*, p. 100.

20. Quoted in *Plea for Liberty*, p. 262.
21. Pp. 192–93.
22. My italics.
23. *Tradition of Freedom*, p. 199.
24. Quoted in *Cahiers du Rhône*.
25. *Plea for Liberty*, p. 247.—Indeed, what self-respecting man has not been at least tempted to cheat at the myriad of tests he is supposed to fill out, answer, check, and spend hours on, either by sabotaging the test or by guessing the answers that the tester wants to receive.
26. *Lettre aux Anglais*, p. 205.
27. "Un Surnaturalisme historique," in *L'Espoir des désespérés*, p. 216.
28. *Lettre aux Anglais;* quoted in *Plea for Liberty*, p. 267.
29. " 'Morning coffee in Paris, aperitive at Chandernagor, and dinner in San Francisco'—can you realize it! Oh, in the next inevitable war the flame-thrower tanks will be able to launch their fire at two thousand meters instead of only fifty, your sons' faces will be instantly boiled and their eyes pop out of their orbits. But when peace is signed, you will again congratulate each other on mechanical progress." *La France contre les Robots*, pp. 137–38.
30. "Un Surnaturalisme historique," etc. p. 208.